Refuge in Hell

Refuge in Hell

Finding God in Sing Sing

Rev. Ronald D. Lemmert

ORBIS BOOKS
Maryknoll, New York 10545

Founded in 1970, Orbis Books endeavors to publish works that enlighten the mind, nourish the spirit, and challenge the conscience. The publishing arm of the Maryknoll Fathers and Brothers, Orbis seeks to explore the global dimensions of the Christian faith and mission, to invite dialogue with diverse cultures and religious traditions, and to serve the cause of reconciliation and peace. The books published reflect the views of their authors and do not represent the official position of the Maryknoll Society. To learn more about Maryknoll and Orbis Books, please visit our website at www.maryknollsociety.org.

Cover art: Debra Classen, *The Annunciation*.

Published by Orbis Books, Box 302, Maryknoll, NY 10545-0302.

Biblical quotations are from the New Revised Standard Version.

Manufactured in the United States of America.
Manuscript editing and typesetting by Joan Weber Laflamme.

NOTE: The characters described in this book are composite characters whose names have been altered. All of the events described, however, actually happened.

Library of Congress Cataloging-in-Publication Data

Names: Lemmert, Ronald D., author.
Title: Refuge in hell : finding God in Sing Sing / Ronald D. Lemmert.
Description: Maryknoll : Orbis Books, 2018.
Identifiers: LCCN 2018004157 (print) | LCCN 2018021783 (ebook) | ISBN 9781608337507 (e-book) | ISBN 9781626982840 (pbk.)
Subjects: LCSH: Church work with prisoners. | Prisoners—Religious life. | Lemmert, Ronald D. | Sing Sing Correctional Facility.
Classification: LCC BV4340 (ebook) | LCC BV4340 .L46 2018 (print) | DDC 259/.5—dc23
LC record available at https://lccn.loc.gov/2018004157

To all of the priests, seminarians, sisters, and laypeople
who have so generously volunteered their time
to share in the mission of proclaiming liberty to captives
by helping to create a refuge within the wasteland of prison.

The spirit of the LORD GOD is upon me,
   because the LORD has anointed me;
he has sent me to bring good news to the oppressed,
   to bind up the brokenhearted,
to proclaim liberty to the captives
   and release to the prisoners,
to proclaim the year of the LORD's favor,
   and the day of vengeance of our God. (Isaiah
      61:1–2)

   —The First Reading at my Ordination Mass

Contents

Foreword

After reading Father Ron's *Refuge in Hell,* I was reminded of Dante's words from *The Divine Comedy:*

> Midway in the journey of my life, I found myself in a dark wood where the straightway was lost. To tell about that wood is hard—so tangled and rough and savage that thinking of it now renews the fear: death is hardly more bitter. . . .
>
> And yet, to treat the good I found there as well I'll tell what I saw.

Father Ron takes us on a journey through the hell of Sing Sing Prison and shares not only what he saw, but also what he experienced at a very deep spiritual level. Through a window he has created, we have an authentic view of what a committed chaplain encounters on a daily basis. He also takes us with vivid insight into the oasis created through a ministry that is deeply sacramental and pastoral. He helps us realize that the human struggle in prison is painful and deep, and that it holds both death and life for the prisoner and the chaplain.

Over the past fifty years I have worked with hundreds of chaplains of all faiths as a fellow chaplain, regional coordinator, and acting director of Ministerial and Family Services. I often have visited worship services and walked with chaplains through the yard, school, visiting room, solitary confinement, hospital, and cell blocks. One didn't have to walk far in order to discover which chaplains were among the "special ones." I believe this book is testimony to the fact that the "oasis" Father Ron helped to create along with the prisoners was a gift to Sing Sing.

We are fortunate to have this deeply spiritual written record by one of the "special ones." However, we can never forget what Nelson Mandela said shortly after his release: "Even when you are treated well, prison is a terrible place to be."

—Rev. Edward Muller

Introduction

Every day, we put our leftover garbage outdoors in a large trash can. Once a week it is taken away, and we forget all about it, never thinking about what happens to it afterward. Many people think of prison in much the same way: a place for disposing society's garbage. Once the dump gets filled, we simply build another. No one ever worries about what happens to the "garbage." The most fulfilling years of my life, however, were spent working in one of those "dumps." I began that career in 1988 as a volunteer at Sing Sing Correctional Facility in Ossining, New York.

After two years of volunteering there, I spent a year as a chaplain at Westchester County Jail in Valhalla, New York, before being hired at Sing Sing. In addition, for the last three of my sixteen years at Sing Sing, I also served as chaplain at the nearby Bedford Hills maximum security prison for women. I always tried to treat my parishioners in prison the same way I would treat any other parishioner: with love and respect, recognizing their dignity as children of God.

Some people approach prison ministry as an opportunity to bring religion to the "godless heathens" and somehow try to get them to "accept" God. Early in my ministry I learned from listening to people's stories that the Divine Presence was already in their midst. God was present in their brokenness, much as God was present in the Suffering Servant in Isaiah:

For he grew up before him like a young plant,
    and like a root out of dry ground;
he had no form or majesty that we should look
        at him,
    nothing in his appearance that we should desire
        him.
He was despised and rejected by others;
    a man of suffering and acquainted with infir-
        mity;
and as one from whom others hide their faces
    he was despised, and we held him of no ac-
        count. (Is 53:2–3)

Mother Teresa recognized the Divine Presence in the beggars dying in the gutters of Calcutta. I came to see my role as helping the rejects from society in prison to recognize that Presence within their own broken lives, so they could see how God had been with them all along, helping them to survive the horrendous nightmares of the past. I wanted them to know that God was eager to help them put the pieces of their shattered lives back together. I didn't go into the prison to bring God; I went there to find God. And I surely did. Ministry is not a one-way street. I experienced the love of God in those broken individuals just as much as they experienced that love in me. This was especially evident shortly after I began working at Sing Sing. At the time I was going through the horrible ordeal of whistleblowing about the pastor of my former parish because some of the boys complained to me about being sexually abused by him. Many of the members of that parish, as well as many of my fellow priests, ostracized me for taking such an unpopular position. But my greatest consolation during those difficult years came from my community behind bars. Through their unwavering support, God sustained me. It was only because of that family behind bars and the grace of God working through them that I did not leave the priesthood during that time of disillusionment.

Over the years we had numerous volunteers and other guests who came in contact with Our Lady of Hope Chapel in Sing Sing. As they interacted with the many different and colorful characters who made up the congregation, all of the volunteers were as amazed as I was to discover the Divine Presence in that chapel behind bars. This book was written at the urging of numerous friends, both inside and outside of prison, to provide a glimpse of how "the Word became flesh" (John 1:14) in the lives of my beloved family behind bars.

While writing this book an old gospel song from my Baptist upbringing played over and over in my mind every day for months: "I Love to Tell the Story." The story that I love to tell is about God's eagerness to forgive sinners. It was my privilege to witness that liberating love at work in the lives of prisoners behind the walls of one of our nation's most notorious maximum-security prisons. Time after time I witnessed the impact of that love on the lives of people who had committed every kind of crime imaginable. This book tells the story of how God's love provides a refuge in whatever hell a person may be experiencing at the moment. It is my prayer that this story about the love of God for prisoners may help the readers of this book find that same refuge in their lives.

Prison "Lingo"

For those readers who are not familiar with prison lingo, the following glossary will make it easier to understand terminology that is unique to prison life:

Bit: A prison sentence. Commonly used to describe doing the sentence "bit by bit" or doing a "bit of time."

Code blue: Prison lockdown. Prisoners immediately have to drop everything and return to their cells for an indeterminate length of time.

Deps: Deputy superintendents. Among others, these include the following:

DSP: The deputy superintendent of programs (my supervisor)

DSS: The deputy superintendent of security. Under the DSS are
COs, corrections officers, supervised by
block sergeants, supervised by
lieutenants, supervised by
captains.

Exec Team: The administrators who run the prison. This team comprises the superintendent (formerly known as a warden) and the first deputy, who is the second in command.

Gallery officer: The officer in charge of all the cells on one gallery.

Housing blocks: The prison is divided into different housing blocks, called A Block, B Block, 5 Building, and the Honor Block. Each block consists of several galleries of cells.

ICP: Intermediary Care Program, a residential psychiatric unit, where some of the mentally impaired prisoners live and receive ongoing treatment.

Keep lock: Being confined to one's cell for twenty-three hours a day for disciplinary purposes.

OIC: The officer in charge of a particular unit.

PSU: Psychiatric Satellite Unit, for acute care.

SHU: Special Housing Unit (the Box), the disciplinary unit, formerly known as solitary.

Tree jumper: Child molester.

1

Volunteering
in the AIDS Unit

Shortly after my assignment to the parish of Holy Name of Mary in Croton-on-Hudson in 1988, our staff invited a Franciscan sister to speak to our youth group about her work with prisoners at Sing Sing who were dying of AIDS. My mother was visiting from the Midwest, so I brought her with me to the presentation. Much to my embarrassment, only one teenager showed up. I apologized to the sister and asked her if she would like to cancel, but she said, "No, because even if only one person hears this message, I am happy." With my mother and me, that made an audience of three, so she was triply happy. She showed a video that had been made in the prison and spoke about what it is like to die of such a dreaded disease while locked up in prison. I was so moved by her presentation that I asked her if she needed any help. I was interested, not because I necessarily wanted to work with prisoners, but because I wanted to work with dying people. My father had recently died a long, painful death, and the hospital chaplain at Mayo Clinic in Rochester, Minnesota, had ministered to him and to our whole family with such care throughout the whole ordeal that I was in-spired to follow his example.

Since the prison was only ten minutes from my parish, I went there on my day off each week to celebrate mass in the hospital dayroom with prisoners with AIDS who were essentially on death row, although this was a death row without possibility of pardon or reprieve. There was a rapid changeover among the patients there. Almost every week someone died and was immediately replaced by another and yet another. Most of our masses were memorial services, since the men were unable to attend the actual funeral services of their comrades. There were very few treatment options at this time, so little could be done for them. It was also a time of great hysteria. People were as afraid of those with AIDS as people from ancient times were afraid of those with leprosy. Most of the nurses who worked there were reluctant to even touch the men. They would hide in their locked office looking busy, rarely coming out except to administer medications or take vitals. A few brave prisoners had the unglamorous tasks of feeding the AIDS-afflicted men, helping them dress, and changing their soiled linens and diapers.

One of these assigned caregivers was Isaac, who, as a troubled youth, had killed a man and was now serving a life sentence. Isaac truly believed his mission in life was to care for these unfortunate rejects of society, and he did so with great love and tenderness right up until their last breath. Many times he stayed up all night with a dying man so he wouldn't have to die alone. The men were always happy whenever Isaac was on duty, because he would give massages. Many of them experienced extreme pain from neuropathy, but Isaac's soothing touch eased their pain and reduced their stress. The Catholic chaplain at that time was an elderly priest who wouldn't even set foot in the unit. If anyone wanted to receive communion, he would meet him at the entrance to the unit and very reluctantly and carefully, out of fear of being contaminated, put the consecrated host into the prisoner's mouth. That was the only contact he had with those dying men, which was why the nun came from a nearby facility once a week to provide some spiritual consolation.

During the two years that I volunteered there, my whole attitude toward prisoners changed. Instead of lumping them all together, I discovered, first of all, that they are not garbage. Every one of them is an individual with a painful story of how he ended up there. As I got to know them, many of them poured out their hearts to me, sometimes in confession, often simply in ordinary conversation. Hearing their stories affected me profoundly. I began to see that nobody sets out in life to become a criminal. There is a whole series of events, along with some poor choices, that lead a person to Sing Sing. In some cases they never had a chance at a normal life from day one. Most of them came from broken and highly dysfunctional families. Many had parents who were alcoholics and/or drug addicts. Many had been badly abused. Few of them had any positive role models or had received good moral guidance. Although there were some who came from good families with plenty of opportunities to do well, for some reason—and there was always a reason—they ended up making some bad choices. They didn't start out by robbing banks and killing people. They didn't even start out by getting high. But teenage rebellion coupled with poor communication and lack of understanding gradually caused their relationship with their parents to deteriorate, while negative peer pressure led them on their way to hell. The discovery of alcohol and drugs only hastened them on the journey. Had they been able to resolve their problems earlier, they wouldn't have felt the need to get high and then wouldn't have committed the crimes that led to prison.

A couple of years before I started volunteering at Sing Sing, the Franciscan sister arranged for Mother Teresa to visit the unit. This was naturally a thrilling experience for everyone in the whole facility. When Mother Teresa saw those dying men, she was over-whelmed with compassion and remarked to the superintendent: "These men should not have to die in prison. I would like to bring them to a hospice in Manhattan to be cared for by members of my community." The superintendent told her that would be impossible; only the governor would be able to release them from prison. "Then let's call the governor," she insisted. The superintendent immediately put in a call to Governor Mario Cuomo and put Mother Teresa on the phone. When she told Governor Cuomo about her plan, to everyone's amazement he agreed, and four men were sent to the newly opened Gift of Love Hospice where they were able to die in peace a few days later.

Not long after I began volunteering at the AIDS unit at Sing Sing, I met Raymond, a young man who, before coming to prison, had been a drug addict trying to find his next fix. When his friendly neighborhood drug dealer refused to give him drugs on credit Raymond got angry, and he returned later to burn down the dealer's apartment. Unfortunately, he burned the wrong apartment, killing a woman along with several little children. Raymond was tormented with guilt, telling me over and over that he didn't mean to hurt that family. This was one of many instances where the sacrament of reconciliation (confession) had a miraculous effect, easing his guilt and allowing him to die in peace.

Then there was Tommy. He was from a wonderful family, with a fine Catholic upbringing. He had been an altar boy throughout school before discovering drugs. From then on his life became a nightmare. Although he had a good relationship with his family, his father was a retired police captain and was too embarrassed to visit his son in prison. Fortunately, Tommy was transferred to an outside hospital toward the end of his illness, and his father was finally able to bring himself to visit his son before he died.

The sister had permission to bring in food for birthday parties, which were always grand celebrations. A Hispanic man named Arturo said that this was the only time in his life that anyone had celebrated his birthday. The following week he was dead. We also celebrated Thanksgiving with roast turkey and all the trimmings that the sister was able to bring into the unit. We began, however, with mass. During the Prayer of the Faithful the men offered their own petitions. A young man named Bobby said, "Lord, I know you hung out with thieves when you were on the cross, so I ask you to hang out with us thieves and lead us to heaven."

At the end of the mass the men were asked to say what they were thankful for. I was totally unprepared for what Bobby said: "I am thankful for having AIDS, because if I didn't, I would never have come to this unit and would never have discovered what it means to be loved."

One of the other volunteers, a layman named Bob, told us the heartbreaking story of how his grandson had been kidnapped by the child's father and taken to South America. He asked the men in the unit to pray for his grandson's safe return. One day, when one of the men was close to death, Bob reminded him, "When you get to heaven and see Jesus, ask him to help me find my grandson." The man died shortly afterward. The next day Bob got a call from the police informing him that they had found his grandson. That incident made a deep impression on all of us, showing the connectedness we share as people of faith, whether in or out of prison. Bob was not a prisoner. There were many differences between him and a man in prison dying of AIDS. But Bob realized that faith was a far greater bond than anything that divided them, so he asked for that dying prisoner's prayers, and we truly believe it was those prayers, coupled with the prayers of countless others, that brought his grandson home.

These experiences changed my life. Before working in the prison, I tended to be very set in my views. If I thought about prisoners at all, it was with contempt. They had broken the law and deserved to be punished. I never gave them another thought. But my involvement in the Respect Life movement had already prompted me to rethink many issues, particularly after Cardinal Joseph Bernardin described his "seamless garment" vision of respecting all forms of life "from the womb to the tomb." That included the incarcerated. They were part of God's family too, and as a fellow member of that family, I needed to show some compassion for them. The stories of these dying men at Sing Sing touched my heart and often moved me to tears. I believe they made me more human. They certainly made me a better Christian and a better priest.

2

The Calling

After only a year of volunteering at Sing Sing, I requested permission from the Archdiocese of New York to become a prison chaplain. Although my preference was always to go to Sing Sing, I would have been willing to accept a position in any prison. But when I developed some serious health issues, I requested a temporary postponement of my assignment request. After that I became so involved in my parish responsibilities at Holy Name of Mary Church in Croton-on-Hudson that my interest in prison work was put on hold. After a few years in that parish as the associate pastor I celebrated my fifteenth year of ordination and I began thinking about applying to become the pastor of another parish. I had considered reapplying to become a prison chaplain but had erroneously heard via the grapevine that those positions were going only to deacons due to the ever-worsening shortage of priests. I applied for two different parishes and was turned down for both because someone with more seniority had applied. But then one night I had a vivid dream in which men from Sing Sing were reaching out to me and calling me by name: "Father Ron, come and help us." The dream was so startling that I immediately woke up, thinking someone was actually calling me. But it was the middle of the night, so I went back to sleep. Over the next few days, however, I was unable to get that dream out of my mind.

Without knowing about my dream, Sister Betty, one of my co-workers in the parish, said: "Ever since you got involved in prison ministry, and whenever you talk about it, you come alive. Since you enjoy that form of ministry so much, why don't you think about becoming a full-time chaplain? Perhaps that is your calling." Suddenly it made sense. This was where God wanted me to be.

So, once again, I requested a prison assignment and asked Ken Hoffarth, the layman in charge of the Archdiocesan Office of Criminal Justice who was responsible for the prison apostolate, about Sing Sing. "We have been eager to get a new man in there for a long time," he replied. "But even though the current chaplain is well into his seventies, he doesn't want to retire yet. We tried to get the administration to help us remove him, but it insisted that he is doing a wonderful job and that everybody loves him. Meanwhile, there is a half-time position available at Westchester County Jail. Would you be interested in that?" I readily accepted the offer and began working part-time at the jail in September 1994, while continuing to live and work part-time in my parish in Croton.

Both men and women are sent to the county jail immediately after their arrest. Unless they get out on bail, they remain there until their trial. If they are exonerated, they go home. If they are convicted, they go back to the jail until after their sentencing. If they are sentenced to less than a year, they will be housed in the penitentiary section of the jail, which is segregated from the non-sentenced prisoners. For any sentence more than a year they are sent to a state prison. If sentenced to more than six years they go to a maximum-security prison like Sing Sing.

The Westchester County Jail had no chapel or any large space available for everyone to worship together. That meant that every day of the week I celebrated Sunday mass in a different unit of the jail, including the women's unit. I would arrive in the afternoon and visit anyone who had requested counseling. Then, in the evening I would celebrate mass in a tiny room next to the law library with anywhere from five to twenty people. A large number of them were Hispanic and spoke very little English, so my homilies needed to be bilingual. I had studied Spanish in the seminary but hadn't had many opportunities to use it in almost twenty years, so I was very rusty and needed some help. Roxie, a good friend of mine from my parish, was originally from Madrid and taught Spanish in high school, so she volunteered to prepare a Spanish translation each week. In addition, she tutored me to help me regain my ability to speak the language. Most of my parishioners, however, were from Latin America, and some of the words she used sometimes had different meanings in different countries with some comical results. On one occasion I had used the term *weird,* which Roxie translated as *bicho raro,* a perfectly legitimate term in Madrid. But as soon as the Latinos heard it, they roared with laughter. "Padre, never use that word!" They explained that it was a very crude reference to a penis.

I kept the homilies simple and brief, reassuring the men and women that in spite of what they may have done, God would never stop loving them. The homilies always were open ended, leading the congregation into a group discussion. They needed not only to hear what I was saying, but to have an opportunity to articulate their thoughts. Many had some terrible misconceptions about God that could only be corrected when they were expressed. "When I was in Catholic school," complained Danny, "Sister Mary always told me that I was no good. So did my parents. I grew up believing that God was angry with me because of it, and now that I am here in jail, this seems to be proof of it." These frank discussions helped me understand my parishioners better, so I could address their needs in the discussion as well as in future homilies. Sharing their

personal stories and interacting with one another helped them to
bond together as a community and provided mutual prayer support
while going through trial and awaiting sentencing.

SOME INDIVIDUAL STORIES

Brian: Learning to Pray

Shortly after my arrival Brian, nineteen years old, asked to see me.
When we sat down in the conference room I asked him what he
wanted to discuss.

"Father Ron, my mom never had me baptized, so I was thinking
that now that I'm locked up this would be a good time to take care
of that."

"You know, Brian," I explained, "baptism is not something that
you just 'take care of'; it is a conversion to a new way of life. Are
you willing to make some changes in the way you live?" I knew that
he was a drug addict with a long list of offenses.

"Yeah, sure," Brian said. "I know I have to stop using drugs and
start going to church. That's why I wanna get baptized."

I wasn't sure we could arrange a baptism in that setting, but I
began meeting with him on a weekly basis to find out more about
him and to give him some badly needed religious education.

After a few weeks Brian appeared a little frustrated. When I
asked him what was wrong, he said, "I was just wondering, when
you gonna teach me 'the prayer'?" I had no idea what he meant until
he explained, "You know, the prayer that will help me beat this rap
so I can get out of jail!"

I tried to explain: "Prayer isn't magic. Getting baptized or learning a particular prayer is no guarantee that you will win your case.
Lots of good people throughout history have experienced all kinds
of injustices. Being a Christian doesn't make you immune to that,

but I can guarantee you that God will always be with you and help you cope with whatever may happen every step of the way."

That was obviously not what he wanted to hear, and that was the last I saw of him.

Alvin and Josh: My Naivete

I was extremely gullible, always presuming people were telling me the truth. One day as I was making rounds in the jail, I came across Alvin and Josh from Atlanta, Georgia. When they mentioned that they were army buddies and Vietnam vets, I let them know I had also been in the army during the Vietnam era, so we swapped a few "war stories."

Josh then explained how they had gotten arrested: "Alvin and I came up here on vacation and picked up a hitchhiker along the way. When we got stopped for speeding the officer made us get out of the car, and when the hitchhiker got out the officer found a package of marijuana on him. We had no idea he had it on him, but we all got arrested for dealing drugs. We are flat broke and cannot pay the $200 bail, so here we sit."

I believed him and felt sorry for them, so I posted their bail. They had promised to repay me, but I never heard from them again.

Joe: Another Test of My Gullibility

I have a soft spot in my heart for both military veterans and cops, so I always gave them special attention in all of my parishes. When I met Joe in the Protective Custody Unit and discovered that he had been a cop in a nearby town, I made a point of getting to know him.

Joe had first been in the New Beginnings drug program (detailed below) until he was spotted by one of the men he had arrested, which then put his life in danger. Since residents of the Protective

Custody Unit are not allowed to attend chapel services, I visited him in his unit on a regular basis to bring him communion. During our numerous one-on-one sessions he told me about his experience as a prisoner of war in Vietnam.

"Our captors were monsters and went out of their way to torture us, both physically and mentally," he told me. "I will never forget watching them play Russian roulette with us, placing one bullet in the chamber, spinning it, then placing the barrel against a man's temple and pulling the trigger, going from one prisoner to another until the gun fired. I haven't been the same since. When I came home I got addicted to drugs, but after getting clean I got a job as a local policeman. Just recently, when my wife left me, I relapsed and started selling drugs to support my habit, which is how I ended up in here."

I was mesmerized by his story and so overcome with sympathy for him that I tried to help him get admitted to a Catholic halfway house where he could get the treatment he needed for his addiction and find an opportunity to make a fresh start in life.

I talked about his case with my long-time friend John, who started to get suspicious.

"Where did you say he was on the police force?" he asked.

When I told him the name of the town, John replied, "You must be talking about Joe, but he was never in Vietnam. He was in my National Guard unit, and we never left New York State."

John also knew the chief of police from the town where Joe had been on the force. The chief helped me sort out fact from fiction. Once again, I had been duped. The only truth in Joe's story was that he had been a cop and was a drug addict. Everything else was bogus.

Roger and Susan: The Complications of Spousal Abuse

About the same time I met Roger, a seemingly very nice guy who had been arrested for an altercation with his wife, Susan. He asked me to call her and let her know he was sorry.

To my amazement, when I called her, Susan said: "Oh, Father, thank you so much for calling me. I am so worried about Roger. It was such a silly little misunderstanding, and I overreacted. Please tell him I am so sorry and am dropping the charges so he can come home."

Shortly afterward Roger was released.

A couple of months later Roger was back in jail due to another altercation with his wife. This time he told me he had a drinking problem that led to temper flare-ups. I suggested he deal with his alcohol problem and offered to take him upon his release to the nearby St. Christopher's Inn, an alcohol rehab run by the Graymoor Friars of the Atonement in Garrison. He agreed to go, but the day after his arrival he called Susan, who came and picked him up. Within weeks he was back in jail.

As we talked about it, Roger acknowledged that he had a problem: "Whenever I am around Susan, she seems to trigger a chemical reaction inside of me. She keeps on badgering me until I explode. I just can't control myself."

This was shortly after the OJ Simpson case in California, so I tried to impress upon Roger the seriousness of the situation and that he needed to stay away from her and to perhaps move far away. He readily agreed, saying, "I have a friend in Chicago who could help me get a job and make a new beginning, but I don't know how I'm going to get there." I offered to buy him a train ticket, for which he was grateful. On the day of his release I picked him up and drove him to the train station. But a week after his arrival in Chicago he called Susan, who immediately sent him money for a return trip. As soon as he returned they had another fight, and that time he knocked out her teeth, broke her jaw, and almost killed her. After she was released from the hospital I saw her at the jail visiting her beloved abuser. Her face was a mess, yet she tried once again to drop the charges. This time, however, due to the public outcry over the Simpson case, the district attorney picked up the charges and proceeded to trial. I never heard what happened afterward, because that was when I transferred to Sing Sing, but I presume Roger was put away for a long time.

Maria: Discovering God's Unconditional Love

One evening I was celebrating mass in the women's unit of the jail when Maria, a young woman who had just arrived that day, came to the service. Maria was distraught and cried softly throughout the entire mass. During the Prayer of the Faithful, when the women customarily offered their personal petitions, Maria tearfully implored us, "Please pray for me, because I want to kill myself."

After mass I spent over an hour counseling her. Maria related how she had come to this country with her husband from the Dominican Republic. "Shortly after our arrival, our son was born and my husband abandoned us. I haven't seen or heard from him since. But I got a job cleaning houses and eventually was able to go to nursing school. After getting a nursing position in a hospital I was finally starting to get ahead in life."

I congratulated her on such an impressive accomplishment.

"But then," she continued, "my ten-year-old son started playing hooky from school. I tried to impress upon him the importance of getting an education, but he wouldn't listen. Yesterday, I was so angry with him that I spanked him. Today he told his friends about it, and they told him to call 911 and report me to Child Protective Services. When I got home from work this afternoon they were waiting for me, and here I am."

In her state of shock Maria reasoned: "Because I am in jail, I must be a very bad mother, and if I am so bad, God must not love me anymore. That is why I no longer want to live. My son must hate me, so he will probably be better off without me."

I asked her if she still loved her son. She was shocked at my question, replying, "Of course I love him. He is my son."

I told her, "If you are capable of loving your son after what he just did, how could you possibly think that God would ever stop loving you?"

Maria had no idea that God's love is unconditional, so I hastened to reassure her. "Even if we don't feel loved at the moment, there is absolutely nothing we could ever do to make God stop loving us. Our feelings can vary from one moment to another, but God's love will always be there."

When I was certain Maria would be all right, I let her go back to her unit. The next day all charges against her were dropped, and she and her son were reunited. Hopefully they both learned something from the ordeal.

NEW BEGINNINGS

The county jail had a drug rehab program called New Beginnings, where I spent a good portion of my time. Working with addicts in recovery and speaking with the addiction counselors on staff provided a wonderful opportunity for me to learn about a whole new world of addiction and recovery. I previously had little patience with addicts, my only contact with them having been limited to the ones who came to the rectory door looking for a handout. But at about the same time I started working in the county jail, I had an experience that changed my attitude. One Sunday morning, between masses, a young man came to the rectory door and asked, "Please, sir, could I talk with you for a few minutes?"

Sunday mornings are quite hectic around rectories, so my initial impulse was to tell him to make an appointment during the week. But he looked so forlorn that I asked, "What would you like to discuss?"

"I am a drug addict," he replied, but hastily added, "I am not looking for money. I just want someone to pray with me so I can stop using drugs."

How could I refuse? I invited him in, placed my hands on his head, and began to pray. Immediately, he collapsed on the floor in a faint. I had no idea what to do, but fortunately he regained consciousness within a couple of minutes. He got up off the floor and. still in a daze, stumbled out the door. A few moments later, when I went next door to the church, that same man walked up to me in the vestibule, threw his arms around me, and said, "Thank you, sir, you just saved my life." I have never seen him since and have no idea what became of him, but that experience changed my life.

Saint Francis of Assisi had a similar experience when a leper helped him overcome his revulsion toward lepers. When he embraced a leper, whom he would have previously avoided, he found that he had embraced Christ. That was how I felt about this drug addict. The conversion of my former attitude needed to take place before I could work in a prison. The New Beginnings program in the Westchester County Jail not only had a plentiful supply of "lepers" to embrace, but it also provided me with many valuable tools that I would need to work with addicts, who make up the majority of the prison population.

Mary: The Slippery Slope to Addiction

At the end of one of our Friday evening masses in the women's unit of the county jail, one of the more elderly prisoners asked me to visit a new arrival who had been unable to attend. When I got to her cell, I was appalled by what I saw. Mary was a middle-aged woman who was detoxing from heroin. She was lying on the floor writhing in pain and shaking convulsively. I had never witnessed anything so horrible in my life. "Thank you so much for coming to see me," she said over and over. But mostly she just babbled incoherently. The brain of a detoxing person is running on overdrive, making it impossible to carry on a coherent conversation. But in the midst of her hot and cold sweats and convulsive shakes she pleaded, "Please, Father, pray for me! I can't do this by myself. Ask God to help me get through this."

I then laid my hands on her head and prayed, "Lord Jesus, you are the Great Physician. You know Mary, and you love her. Please lay your healing hands upon her and set her free from this addiction. Ease the pain of withdrawal and give her peace."

The following week Mary came to mass. She still wasn't completely over her withdrawal symptoms and hadn't slept the whole week, but coming to mass was extremely important to her, and she became one of our regulars. Little by little her story unfolded. Unlike most of the others, she was well educated and came from a staunch Irish Catholic family. "I was the primary caregiver for my mother while she was dying of cancer," she explained, "and I completely fell to pieces after her death. Because I was a nurse administrator in a hospital in Manhattan I had relatively easy access to drugs and quickly discovered that when I took a painkiller, my problems became more manageable. But it wasn't long before I was addicted, got fired, lost my house here in Westchester, and eventually was living on the streets and eating out of garbage cans while prostituting myself to support my heroin habit. Actually, Father, getting arrested and coming to jail saved my life. I am much better off in here now than I was a few weeks ago on the streets."

I would later discover that Mary's story was not unique. Nobody starts out as a full-fledged addict living on the streets. Most start out as recreational drug users. Education, financial status, or social standing do not make one immune to the diabolical force of addiction. Although not everyone who experiments with drugs ends up a junkie, all junkies started down that slippery slope by experimenting with something that they thought would make them feel better. The jail was filled with people who had once thought they had their "recreational drug usage" under control.

It was while I was working in the county jail and listening to the tragic stories of people going through its seemingly revolving door because of their addictions that I began to develop a plan to open a halfway house. I discussed it with some of the men as well as with the staff of New Beginnings to see if there would be any interest. Their answer was a resounding yes, so I put together a board of directors and began making plans for the future. It would be called My Father's House, because it would be purchased with money I had inherited from my father.

Pat: One Moment in Time

I was very energized by my work in the county jail. I found it particularly interesting to read about a high-profile case in the local newspaper one day and then meet the suspect the next day in the jail. People were always in a state of crisis as they awaited their fate. Such was the case with Pat, a young man who was convicted of murder.

After Pat's initial arrest he was out on bail on house arrest. But once he was convicted, he was brought to the jail. I went to see him the next day.

"Hello, Pat," I greeted him. "I've been following your case in the newspaper. I know you come from a Catholic family, so I've been eagerly waiting to meet you. Would you like to get out of this cell and talk with me?"

When he readily agreed, I got permission from the guard to take him to a conference room where we could talk privately.

I began the conversation by saying, "I know the newspapers like to sensationalize everything to sell papers, but perhaps you could tell me what really happened."

"To this day," Pat explained, "I have absolutely no recollection of what happened. It was five years ago, and I was in an alcoholic blackout. The last thing I remember was getting drunk with my friends and then cracking up my car on the way home. The next morning I woke up stark naked in my bed. I have no idea what happened to my clothes. Then the police called and said they had my car, but it never even occurred to me that I might have killed someone.

"My car crash was a wake-up call for me. I realized that my drinking was out of control. I had had a problem with alcohol since I was a teenager, so I made the decision to get some help and started going to AA. As my mind started to clear, I began having nightmares about a murder that were so disturbing that I confided in my friends in AA, wondering if there could possibly be a connection with a long unsolved murder in town. One of them informed the police, who then brought me in for questioning and fingerprinting. The fingerprints matched, I was arrested, and here I am."

To look at such a case as an outsider and know only what had been presented in the media, one would have believed the young man to be a budding Jack the Ripper. But after meeting him and hearing his story, I saw that there was far more to this person than those grisly actions committed at that one isolated moment in time. I counseled him for the four months he was at the county jail and also brought in a retired psychologist as a chapel volunteer to counsel him. Although Pat had no recollection of what he had done, he knew he must have done it, since his bloody palm print had been found at the scene. He was horrified to realize the damage he had inflicted on the family of his victim.

I grew very close to Pat during that time and volunteered to speak at his sentencing. I had never been in a courtroom before, so I did not realize that the defendant's family sat on one side while the victim's family sat on the other. I sat on the wrong side in the midst of a large group of very hurt and angry people. When given an opportunity to give a victim's impact statement, they tearfully spoke of the disastrous impact this crime had had on their family and ridiculed the idea that Pat could possibly have any sense of remorse for what he had done.

When I came forward to speak on Pat's behalf, everyone around me glared furiously while making loud hissing sounds and catcalls. I walked up to a podium near the judge's bench and said I was there as Pat's priest at the Westchester County Jail, and as his priest I had seen him from a totally different perspective, which I then shared with them.

I wanted them to know how much he had changed in the four years since that crime had occurred, once the alcohol was out of his system and he had become involved in the Twelve Steps of the Alcoholics Anonymous program. I wanted them to know that he was not a callous, unfeeling monster, but a gentle, sensitive young man who gives me a big hug every time he sees me and kneels on the bare floor after receiving communion to pray that God will help to ease the horrible pain he inflicted upon that family through his crime. I wanted them to know that Pat did not choose to commit this crime. He was incapable of any kind of choice in his sickened condition. He was not trying to deny responsibility for his actions by blaming others. But I asked the court: "What good can come from the maximum sentence? If it is to teach Pat a lesson, his conscience, which he must live with for the rest of his life, is already doing that. If it is to make an example of him so no one else commits a similar crime, why delude ourselves? Anyone in an alcoholic blackout or under the influence of other drugs is not going to think about consequences. Will justice truly be served with 'an eye for an eye and a tooth for a tooth'? That is why I ask that justice be tempered by mercy and compassion. I am not asking for no jail time. I am just asking that he be given less than the maximum."

In spite of my plea for justice tempered with mercy, Pat was given the maximum sentence for manslaughter, two consecutive sentences of eight and one half to twenty-five years.

Pat had made such an impression on me during his stay at the county jail that I have stayed in touch with him from the time he entered the state prison system up to the present. I also talked with his chaplains and was always happy to hear how well he was doing. Because of his background as a carpenter, his chaplain at Eastern Correctional Facility asked him to help renovate the chapel. The dedication ceremony for the renovated chapel was celebrated by Cardinal Egan. The chaplain had asked me to play the organ and direct the choir for the occasion, so I had an opportunity to see Pat for the first time in several years. I beamed with pride throughout the whole liturgy when I saw him serving on the altar with the cardinal. A few years later he was sent to Sing Sing to participate in the New York Theological Seminary's master's program, where, for a whole year, he was very active in our chapel program and was one of the speakers at two of our retreats.

As his service project for the master's program he chose to work in Sing Sing's residential psychiatric unit, where he interacted with men with serious psychological illnesses. He helped them learn basic skills such as personal hygiene and how to relate better with one another in the unit as well as with others in the general population of the prison. Pat practically adopted one of the men in our chapel who lived on that unit and had the mental capacity of a five-year-old, which made him extremely vulnerable to others who took advantage of him. Pat had the patience of a saint working with him, teaching him how to dress properly and how to behave in public so he could blend in a little better.

No one, including Pat, would condone Pat's actions in the past, when his out-of-control addiction to alcohol led him to commit a horrendous crime. But that one horrible moment doesn't define who Pat is today. He has worked very hard to address his problems and exorcize his demons and in the process of doing so has helped many other people to do the same.

ON TO THE "BIG HOUSE":
SING SING PRISON

One month after I spoke at Pat's sentencing, the elderly chaplain at Sing Sing retired. I was in Illinois at the time, visiting my mother, when Kenneth Hoffarth called from the archdiocese to ask if I would be willing to accept the position. "Ken," I replied, "nobody was ever happier about going to Sing Sing than I am." Unfortunately, due to the state's budget problems they could not employ me immediately, so I continued to work at the county jail but volunteered to celebrate mass at Sing Sing once a week until the state could hire me.

Once I had gotten the word that I would be working at Sing Sing, planning for the halfway house moved at a faster pace. A real estate agent from my parish found an ideal location in Peekskill within walking distance of the Parole Office, Social Services, and public transportation. I could not obtain a mortgage, however, until I got a full-time job. Fortunately, the sale process dragged on just as slowly as the state delayed in hiring me.

Meanwhile, I got my first taste of bureaucratic incompetence while trying to arrange a time to celebrate Sunday mass. Since I was still working at the county jail as well as at the parish in Croton, I had to work around both schedules. But my immediate supervisor at Sing Sing wouldn't budge to accommodate anyone. Neither Saturday nor Sunday in the afternoon or evening was acceptable because of the movie schedule in the auditorium, which was in the same building as the chapel. In later years we frequently had mass while movies were going on in the auditorium, but this was not an option with this supervisor. The only time I could celebrate Sunday mass was at 8:30 on Monday morning.

Previously, when I had volunteered at the AIDS Unit in the prison infirmary, I was always escorted by an officer. Since an escort officer was not always available, I frequently had to wait an hour to get from the front gate to the infirmary. This time, since I was supposed to be hired soon, I was given permission to walk to the chapel unescorted. The only problem was, nobody told me where the chapel was. So, on my first day, after being searched for contraband at the front gate, I walked up several flights of steep steps to the top of the tunnel and looked around to get my bearings. I had no idea where I was going, so I just followed a large group of prisoners heading toward another tunnel. Once we got to the tunnel I could see the chapel straight ahead, so I kept going toward it, even though the prisoners all turned left to enter what I later learned was 5 Building. Unfortunately, when I got there, all of the doors to the chapel were locked, and no one was in sight. So I returned to the previous tunnel and entered the gate to 5 Building, where an officer directed me through two more gates to another tunnel that led to the chapel.

At the entrance to the chapel building was another gate, behind which was a desk where an officer was sitting. He had the key to open and lock the gate that led into a large auditorium. In a wing to the left was the Catholic chapel, and in a wing to the right was the Protestant chapel. The Jewish and Muslim chapels were in the basement, along with a classroom for the New York Theological Seminary's master's program. I had been issued a key ring that held approximately twenty keys of various shapes and sizes. The OIC (officer in charge) showed me which one opened the front door of the Catholic chapel, but I was on my own with the other nineteen keys. Then I met George, an elderly prisoner who had been my predecessor's clerk for ten years.

"Prisoners aren't allowed to touch keys," he explained, "but I can show you which one opens each door or cabinet."

Everything had to be unlocked and then locked again wherever I went, even the telephone in my office. I felt as though I were working in Fort Knox.

I had come prepared for a large crowd of prisoners eager to meet their new chaplain, but there were only six men there. George explained that they had to work during the day. My supervisor had assured me that they would be excused from their duties to attend mass, but he hadn't kept his promise. Not even Tony, who had for years been the altar server in residence, was allowed to come. After we finished the mass a young man approached me and asked if I would hear his confession. I was delighted and took him into the sacristy for privacy, at which point, much to my horror, he asked me, "Do you want me to give you a blow job?" I quickly assured him that I certainly did not and immediately ushered him out the door. I later discovered that he was from the Intermediary Care Program (ICP). He never came back again. For the next five months there were usually only six men at mass, mostly from the ICP.

I was finally hired on September 1, 1995. Then, although I was fully prepared to celebrate mass the following Sunday, the supervisor came to the chapel that morning to inform me he didn't want me to begin mass until after my official orientation, claiming that I was too new and wouldn't know what to do, even though I had already been celebrating Mass there since April. That supervisor had no problem with volunteers of other faiths leading worship services in the other chapels, but he wouldn't allow me to celebrate my first mass as an official New York State Catholic chaplain. Thus began my career of coping with what I would quickly discover was a vehemently anti-Catholic attitude among incompetent bureaucrats who did everything possible to thwart my ministry every step of the way for the next sixteen years. When I was finally allowed to begin celebrating mass, I gave the following homily:

First Sunday at Sing Sing, 1995

I have been wandering around the facility for the past week, trying to find where the various units are located. In my travels, I met a young man who had been away from the church for many years. [*He was in the Psych Unit, but I never mentioned that in the homily in order to protect his identity. His mother had recently died, and he had tried to kill himself.*] As we talked, he told me he didn't think God could ever forgive him for the things he had done, but I told him he was wrong. There is no one God would ever refuse to forgive as long as the person repents. God will never give up on anybody, because God loves us and wants to bring us back into a loving relationship with him.

Today's First Reading illustrates the primitive understanding people had of God's attitude toward sin. When Moses was leading the People of Israel through the desert, they stopped at Mount Sinai, where Moses received the Ten Commandments. He was up on the mountain for forty days, and the people were afraid something had happened to him. They felt abandoned and didn't know what to do. They didn't really know this new God who had gotten them out of Egypt, and they had no idea how to get in touch with God without Moses to intercede for them. So they decided to make a new god in the form of a golden calf to help them find their way out of the desert. This, of course, was a sin. They had failed to trust in the true God and had turned to a false one. So when Moses finally came down from the mountain, he thought God must be very angry with them. He thought God would destroy them for such a terrible sin. That's why he begged God to spare their lives.

From what we know of God today, it would be unthinkable for God to annihilate an entire nation for any reason, and certainly not for losing faith during such a stressful situation. Moses didn't know that back then, but he would quickly discover that God isn't like that. In spite of their sinfulness and lack of faith, God forgave them. He didn't kill them, and he didn't abandon them. They were still God's people whom he loved, and he gave them an opportunity to try again.

Today's Gospel gives us another description of God's desire to forgive. Jesus told a story about a shepherd who goes out in search of his lost sheep. Some might think the shepherd should be content with the other ninety-nine and forget about one lousy stray. But the shepherd didn't stop searching until he found that lost sheep. That is what God is like. The man I mentioned earlier had a saintly mother who never stopped praying for him. Even though she recently died, she's still praying that the Good Shepherd will find her poor lost lamb." [*And he did. Upon release from the Psych Unit that "lamb" returned to the chapel and remained active until his transfer to another facility. He came back briefly for a court hearing a few years later, and when he spotted me in the corridor he came up to me and gave me a big hug and told me how well he has been doing. While he was lost, his life was so dismal he wanted to end it, but once he was found, he discovered meaning and fulfillment and joy—even in prison.*]

If you have ever felt that God would never forgive you, I'd like you to think carefully about these scripture passages and allow them to change your impression of what God is like. I would never think of dedicating my life to a god who cannot forgive or who holds grudges or who doesn't care about those with problems. If your god is like that, maybe it's time to find a new one, and I would like to recommend mine. The only God worth serving is one who loves us and is capable of forgiving anything. If you find it difficult to imagine a God great enough to forgive all your sins, you are placing limits on God and making God considerably less than almighty. So I invite you to let go of any limits you may have placed on God in the past and give God a chance to demonstrate his love and power. I've been waiting six years for the opportunity to come in here and tell you guys how much God loves you. And in the days and years ahead, I will do everything in my power to convince you I'm telling you the truth.

Only twelve men showed up for that first mass. They were delighted that they finally had a chaplain, and Tony reminded me, "Jesus began his ministry with only twelve men, too." Like the original twelve disciples, these men immediately began spreading the word. Shortly after my arrival, the prisoner-leader of the Muslim chapel came up to me and said, "Father Ron, if anyone ever tries to lay a hand on you here, he will be dead," while making a cutting motion across his throat. He wanted me to know that the Muslims had my back.

The Catholic prison chaplains from the Archdiocese of New York met periodically, and when we got together shortly after my assignment at Sing Sing they gave me a hearty welcome. Father Ed Donovan was a legendary figure who had been the chaplain at Green Haven Correctional Facility for over thirty years. I had already met him a few times because I had been a team member on a couple of the retreats he had for his men. He was a colorful character, walking around in his shabby old cassock covered with ashes and an occasional hole from his ever-present cigars. He was revered by his men, feared by the guards, and hated by the administration.

Father Ed took me aside after the meeting and gave me a little fatherly advice: "Never forget that the members of the Exec Team are not your friends. They work for an evil empire that is devoted to destroying the lives of the people we are trying to save. Chaplains must never forget where their allegiance lies. We have to work with the administration in order to get anything done, but chaplains who start getting involved socially with them compromise their integrity and cannot fulfill their intended function in advocating for the prisoners." He also told me that because a chaplain's salary is much greater than the customary salary of a priest, it is the responsibility of the chaplain to support the ministry and to provide the things that the prison won't provide, whether materials for fixing up the chapel, bibles, religious literature, or refreshments for the congregation. I took his advice to heart at the beginning of my chaplaincy, and throughout the years I grew to appreciate the wisdom he had accumulated during his thirty-seven years of battling that evil empire.

3

"Francis, Rebuild My Church"

While most of the newer prisons have one chapel that is shared by everyone, Sing Sing is one of very few prisons in New York State with separate chapels for Protestants, Catholics, Jews, and Muslims. This provided a wonderful opportunity to develop a wide variety of chapel activities. The sanctuary was divided from the rest of the chapel by a large floor-to-ceiling screen that was cranked up for mass and then cranked back down for the rest of the week. George was unable to crank it up; it could only be done when Tony, who was much younger and stronger, was there for mass on Sundays. The sanctuary was crowded with two life-size wooden statues of Mary and the Sacred Heart of Jesus and two life-size plaster statues of Saint Joseph and another of the Sacred Heart. All of them were in very bad shape. The altar had a linoleum top covered with a shabby white cloth. There were no other altar linens in the appropriate colors for the liturgical seasons. Tattered damask curtains hung in shreds behind the altar, and badly damaged green floor tiles were covered with black crud. The space for the congregation was bare, with blue folding theater seats bolted to the concrete floor, which was painted battleship gray.

Everything was dirty and dingy. The old dark-beige and brown paint on the chapel walls was peeling. One corner of a large asbestos ceiling tile had become unglued and was hanging down. And what was going on was unsightly as well. Tony told me, "The officers usually just sat in the back of the chapel and slept while the gangsters conducted business right in front of them during mass. Others would deal drugs, and their customers would periodically leave the chapel to go to the bathroom and get high. Sometimes transvestites would make out with their customers right in the middle of the congregation."

"Sounds like Sodom and Gomorrah," I said.

"That's right," Tony replied. "Everybody knew what was going on in here, and nobody ever did anything about it. Father John would occasionally stop reading his homily long enough to yell at them, but then he would go back to reading and they would get back to business. Through it all, the officers would just take a nice nap and do nothing."

Obviously, there was a need for a lot of changes, and I was eager to get started. George was over seventy years old with numerous health problems. Whenever I told him about an idea for changing the way things were done, his response was, "But we never did it that way." Or he would remind me, "We have to be careful not to let these criminals take advantage of you." His intentions were good, but I knew that things had to change. One of the first things I did was rearrange the office. My immediate task was to make the place look respectable, so people would see right away that things were different, but my overall goal was to rebuild our congregation.

MEETING MY NEW PARISHIONERS

Tony

The chaplain traditionally had worked an 8 a.m. to 4 p.m. shift. That schedule would have to be changed. Most of the men were assigned to various jobs around the facility that required them to work all day. Some were plumbers, carpenters, aides in the school, mess-hall workers, office clerks, or, far more commonly, custodial porters in the housing blocks. But most of them were free during the evening. Tony, the "altar server in residence," was a Fordham graduate and very responsible. Since there were no Catholic events other than Sunday mass, he had gotten permission from the administration long before my arrival to conduct a small group to pray the Rosary and have a Bible discussion every Wednesday evening. I was intrigued by Tony, who didn't look anything like one would expect a convict to look, so I called him into my office to talk. I began the conversation as I would do innumerable times throughout my ministry there: "Tony, how did a nice guy like you end up in a place like this?"

Tony then told me his life story. He had had a good career as an accountant with a New York City agency, but "at a party one night, just for fun, I tried smoking crack cocaine to see what it was like. I had no idea addiction could happen so quickly. After that one time, crack became an obsession. I drained my whole life's savings to keep on smoking more of it. My addiction consumed me. Nothing else mattered. Fortunately, realizing my life was out of control, I chose to retire so as not to be fired and lose my pension. But as my addiction continued to progress, I lost my family, friends, reputation, and home. My whole life came unglued. Eventually, to support my growing habit, I committed a series of robberies and ended up here."

Tony had already been drug free in prison for over five years when I met him. To talk to him, one would imagine him to be a successful lawyer or doctor. His grammar was impeccable. He never cursed or smoked. Once he was free from drugs, he was a dependable, intelligent person who was an invaluable resource, which was why the administration had allowed him to conduct the Bible study without any supervision.

I had one suggestion for him: "Tony, you are a very responsible worker here in the chapel. You are a wonderful altar server and lector, and you are always ready and eager to do anything that needs to be done. However, I think it is important for other people to get involved, so let's try to train some other altar servers and lectors. Do you think you could help me do that?"

"Sure, Father," Tony replied. "There is no need for me to be a one-man show. In the past no one else ever wanted to do anything, which is why I did it all, but times have changed. I'll be glad to help find some other guys and help you train them, too."

Angelo

Angelo, a middle-aged Filipino, was another intriguing fellow who, like Tony, came from a professional background and did not fit the typical Hollywood stereotype of a prisoner. "Angelo," I began, "you seem totally at peace. What is your secret?"

"I was an absolute wreck when I was arrested for manslaughter and ended up in Riker's Island [New York City's largest jail]. That first night I was in a state of shock and terrified of what would be happening. I prayed harder than I had ever prayed before in my life, and while I was praying—you may think I'm crazy, but this is the God's honest truth—I saw Jesus in my cell. He came up to me and comforted me, reassuring me that I would be all right if I would just trust him. Ever since that experience, I have been fine."

Antonio

Antonio, a middle-aged Dominican, spoke only broken English. But he was in the Honor Block with George, and they were inseparable friends. Antonio became one of our Spanish lectors at mass and was very devout. His life before coming to prison was all about escaping from poverty. He came to New York from the Dominican Republic to provide a better life for his family. While living in a Bronx slum, feeding his family was an ongoing struggle. Then one day a fellow Dominican made him a job offer he couldn't resist—runner for a drug dealer. "All I had to do was carry a small package of drugs from one location to another," he explained, "for which I would make far more money than I was making at my custodial job in a warehouse. Life suddenly got much better for us. We were able to move out of the slums to a decent apartment, and finally I could provide some of the finer things in life that we had always dreamed of—until I got busted. My whole world collapsed when I was sentenced to twenty-to-life under the Rockefeller Drug Laws."

George

George was not nearly so open with me. He always kept up his guard and never talked about his personal life. I respected his privacy and tried not to pry, but eventually I discovered that this was his third "bit" (sentence) in prison. All three sentences were for manslaughter and were mob related. This time he would obviously not be getting out alive.

The Greek

Another prisoner, an elderly man called the Greek, spoke very little English but enjoyed fellowship with the others. He had been in a dispute with a fellow immigrant over a business deal. They had quarreled, and in a fit of anger he had stabbed the man to death.

Fred

The most colorful character was an elderly man named Fred. He had serious mental issues, which made it difficult to carry on a conversation with him. Regardless of the subject matter, he always ended up berating his ex-wife at great length. It took several years before I got to the root of his problem, which was that he had murdered their son. But he was in such a state of denial that he was unable to face what he had done. He always told people, "My son committed suicide, and my wife has blamed me for it ever since." Years later, at the closing of one of our retreats, he admitted: "I've always said that my son committed suicide. That is true, but he used me as the weapon. By pushing me so far with his arrogant attitude and harassment, egged on by his mother, who always hated me, I became the gun that he used to kill himself."

That was the closest he could come to acknowledging what had happened. Meanwhile, every discussion and every prayer petition at mass or at the Bible study always revolved around how badly his ex-wife was persecuting him. He drove everybody crazy, but yet, in his own way, he was a lovable character. Even though he was a Lutheran, he preferred to attend our services and was a loyal and faithful participant in all of our chapel activities.

These six men had bonded together as true brothers in Christ. They enjoyed one another's company while praying together and reflecting on the scriptures every Wednesday evening. One of their major prayer intentions was for a renewal of the chapel.

THE BIBLE STUDY GROUP

Once I had gone through the new employees' orientation and was cleared to begin working, I immediately arranged my schedule so I could meet with the Bible study group on Wednesday evenings. At our first meeting Tony explained what they had been doing for the past two years: "We have always read the scripture readings for the following Sunday and then discussed them among ourselves. Then we prayed the Rosary together and shared prayer intentions.

But always," he emphasized, "our main intention was for the Lord to send a more active shepherd to care for this flock of stray sheep. Today we hope that in you God has answered our prayers."

I then told them, "Just about the same time that you started praying for a new shepherd, I had a vivid dream about men from Sing Sing stretching out their arms and saying, 'Father Ron, come and help us.' That is why I am here."

The men all promised me their support and wholehearted co-operation. I suggested that we change the format slightly to begin with mass, followed by the Rosary, and then Bible study with open discussion, and they enthusiastically agreed.

Attendance quickly increased to twelve in the first few weeks. Angelo was a jailhouse gourmet who frequently treated us with homemade cheesecake, pizza, and other goodies that he made in a little hotpot in his cell. I marveled at his ingenuity when he explained how he did it. After removing the upper part of the hotpot, he cut both ends off of a tuna fish can and placed it over the heating coil. Then, a covered sauce pan, purchased on the black market from one of the officers, was placed on top of the tuna fish can to provide a makeshift oven for baking. Tony always brought us coffee, sugar, and creamer. I brought in my two synthesizer keyboards to provide music.

We soon developed into a multipurpose group: mass, Rosary, Bible study, and choir all in one evening. The choir began practicing for Christmas, and the men were thrilled to be able to sing Christmas carols. At one of our first rehearsals Tony asked, "Do you think we could learn to sing *O Holy Night*?" I promised to bring in the music the following week so we could try. It took a lot of work, but they were enthusiastic. Angelo sang the verses as a solo, since he had a clear tenor voice. The others came in on the refrain in two-part harmony. They were a bit rough around the edges and not quite in tune, but I'm sure the heavenly choir was cheering us on.

Before entering the seminary I had spent four years working as the organist-choirmaster at the Catholic chapel at the United States Military Academy at West Point, where I had an eighty-voice, all-male choir of cadets that sang for masses and went on periodic concert tours. Music in the liturgy had always been a major priority in all of my parishes, and this one would be no exception. In the beginning the only musical accompaniment was what I provided on my synthesizers, kept in the sanctuary next to the altar so I could play the hymns we used during mass as I alternated roles between mass celebrant and musician. But over the years some of the men helped me build up quite an impressive musical ensemble with guitars, conga drums, bongos, maracas, tambourines, and a trumpet that some of my friends and relatives generously provided. We eventually outgrew our Wednesday evening time slot and moved our rehearsals to Saturdays, when we had more time. I continued to play the synthesizers with them but also taught them to read music so we could expand our repertoire. As a result, the music in our liturgies became exciting and vibrant.

RENOVATION BEGINS

The story of Saint Francis of Assisi, who heard the Lord call him to rebuild the church, had been my inspiration throughout my parish ministry. That simple vision had brought about profound change in the whole church, so I decided to use that Franciscan theme of rebuilding the church to get the men in the Bible study group involved in fixing up the chapel. I hoped that doing so would help to rebuild their lives. They all realized our rundown, shabby chapel needed a lot of work and were excited about being asked to help. They eagerly volunteered their time and talents and even got some of their non-churchgoing friends involved, and consequently back to church. One of our first projects was to get all the statues out of the sanctuary and place them in the four corners of the outer area around the congregation. We ripped off the tattered curtains and scraped the crud off the tiles.

Shortly before Thanksgiving, Sergeant Coop, who was in charge of the facility's maintenance crew, stopped me in the hallway and asked, "How would you like to have our maintenance crew paint your chapel? It looks pretty drab and hasn't been painted in a long time. We could strip off all of that peeling paint and have it ready for Christmas."

I was delighted by her offer and immediately said yes.

Upon returning to the chapel I relayed the good news to George. As usual, he didn't think it was a good idea. "You just don't understand, Father, that nothing works around here the way it is supposed to. They make promises, but they never keep them. Sergeant Coop is a nice lady, and I'm sure she is trying to make a good impression on you, but make her wait until after the holidays. Otherwise, we will have scaffolds in here for Christmas."

I relayed George's concerns to Sergeant Coop, who reassured me: "Don't worry. My crew has some down time right now, and I give you my word we will start immediately after Thanksgiving and be done in less than a week."

Much to George's dismay, I let him know we were going ahead with the plan. And in doing so, I suddenly felt liberated. I informed him, "We have to get ready for the painters to start next week so we will have to round up a few volunteers to help us move furniture out of the way." George was not happy, fully expecting he would be able to tell me "I told you so" at Christmas. However, he helped me spread the news to the Bible study men, who were glad to help. Sergeant Coop was true to her word, and the whole chapel was finished on time. We painted it white, which brightened things up considerably. It was also the beginning of a wonderful relationship with an amazing woman who helped me accomplish many other renovation projects.

Once the chapel was painted, it was time to start decorating for Christmas. The administration gave me permission to bring in some decorations, since the ones we had were dreadful, and we had a little decorating party. The chapel already had a bedraggled, old artificial Christmas tree, but with some new decorations and lots of lights it looked splendid. We hung candy canes on the tree, but before the evening was over they had all mysteriously disappeared. We also hung a garland and red bows above the crucifix and arranged the manger scene at the foot of the altar. It was very simple—but it was a start and quickly became the talk of the whole prison. Unfortunately, aside from the choir and Bible study group, very few people came to mass on that first Christmas.

Tony explained, "Christmas in prison is so painful that most people would rather pretend it never happened. A few of the guys party in their cell blocks, some get high, but most just stay in their cells and mope."

After Christmas we got back to work cleaning up the chapel. I decided there was no reason to keep the screen down during the week. I got Tony to crank it up and left it up for the remainder of my time at Sing Sing.

"But Father," George warned, "people will come in here and have sex!"

"Over my dead body," I said. "We will simply have to spend more time up here in the chapel supervising the workers. When we can't be here, we will lock the chapel door."

One of our first major jobs was to strip the battleship-gray paint off the floor. That, however, was no easy task, in part because prisoners are not allowed to have tools due to the possibility that they could also be used as weapons. But Tony came up with a brilliant solution: "We can use can tops. We will just bend them in half and use the sharp, round edge to scrape the floor." With those can tops they began the long and tedious process of scraping many layers of paint off the floor, a task that took a few years to complete. Eventually, with the help of Sergeant Coop, we were able to get some paint stripper from the maintenance department, which helped tremendously. Once we got the paint removed, we applied a sealer and many layers of wax that were buffed to a high gloss. It looked magnificent.

It took me a while to figure out how to get supplies from the facility. Anytime I tried to follow the facility rules, the answer was always no. Although six thousand dollars was budgeted for the chapels annually, we got only a few hundred dollars of that to purchase missalettes and candles. The remainder was diverted to other areas (or perhaps pockets). But I eventually discovered that offering maintenance workers a cup of coffee and a few cookies would get me all kinds of things. Being on good terms with Sergeant Coop was also helpful. If she didn't have something I needed, she knew how to pull the necessary strings to get it. In addition, the rabbi knew someone in the city's garment district and was able to get fabric donated for new sanctuary curtains. Then Angelo sewed them by hand in his cell in 5 Building with the permission of the sergeant. Since we had no drapery hangers, he sewed matching loops to fasten the curtains onto the metal frame behind the altar. One of the counselors sewed a new altar cloth. Tony knew someone who worked in maintenance who provided us with an electric sander so we could strip and refinish all of our doors and woodwork. I brought in golden oak stain, which was a vast improvement over the drab brown paint. Soon our broken-down kneelers were repaired and reupholstered, and the light fixtures and the metal framework behind the altar were painted gold. The rabbi got us more material to make draperies to surround our stained-glass windows.

Bloomsburg Carpet Industries, owned by one of my former parishioners in Croton, donated carpeting for the sanctuary. Getting the administration to accept the donation was a challenge. It initially voiced suspicion that the company must have some connection with one of the prisoners in the chapel and that there was some kind of ulterior motive behind the offer. I insisted that I knew the owner of the company, and he was donating the carpeting as a favor for me. Then my supervisor objected because the carpet would get dirty, at which point I reminded him that the Muslim chapel had carpet that was cleaned periodically. Eventually the administration reluctantly gave permission, and the company came in and installed the carpet around the altar area, with beautiful results.

GROUP DISCUSSIONS

That January we got our first four chapel volunteers: Ed, Anne, Pam, and Patrick. Ed was a chaplain at Calvary Hospital, a hospice for people dying of cancer. His wife, Anne, was the academic dean at the nearby Maryknoll Missionary Society's Lay Missioner Program. Pam, a former social worker, had volunteered with me at the women's unit in the county jail. All three of them came from my former parish. Patrick had just retired as a librarian at Fordham University and read in the archdiocesan newspaper that Sing Sing had gotten a new chaplain, so he called to volunteer his services.

They came on Wednesday evenings for our mass and Bible study. They would arrive at 5 p.m. to be screened at the front gate and then had to wait at least an hour to be transported to the chapel. Meanwhile, in the chapel we began with choir practice at 5 p.m. and waited until their arrival at 6:30 p.m. to start the mass. After mass we spent approximately twenty minutes socializing while having coffee and cookies. We brewed our own coffee, so this was a welcome change from the instant coffee in the mess hall. By then our group had expanded to twenty-five and was continuing to grow, so we divided into four small groups with a civilian volunteer to lead each discussion group. One of those groups was devoted to preparing our two candidates, Brandy and Tex, for confirmation, along with their sponsors, who were fellow prisoners. Brandy was a young man with a serious alcohol problem who was in for a DWI (driving while intoxicated). Tex had a much more colorful background as a gang member who had been a pimp for a brothel. I counseled both of them extensively in addition to the Wednesday night instructions.

The format for the group discussions evolved over the next couple of years. I eventually created a series of worksheets based on the scripture readings for the following Sunday's liturgy. Since most of the men would otherwise be hearing those readings for the first time on Sundays, the extra exposure to the scriptures on Wednesdays provided another opportunity for the readings to sink in. When everyone later broke into small discussion groups, they would share how the scripture readings related to their experience in prison.

Here is one of the discussion guides we used:

Feast of the Holy Family
Scripture readings:
Sirach 3:2–14; Colossians 3:12–21; Luke 2:41–52

Focus: Making Our Families Holy
The Feast of the Holy Family is celebrated on the Sunday after Christmas every year to remind us that Jesus did not grow up in a vacuum. He was lovingly cared for and received his spiritual formation within a human family. The roles of

Mary and Joseph in rearing their child so that he could grow into a responsible adult are a reminder of the role of every parent in helping to produce a holy family today.

Discussion Questions

How has your experience of family life helped you or harmed you?

What can you do to make your family more holy today?

What kind of impact is our celebration of Christmas at Sing Sing having on you?

The men enjoyed these small group discussions very much. Since there were five or six men in each group, they had an opportunity to talk openly and to bond with one another. They frequently got off topic, but that was all right. The important thing was that they could be themselves and share their impressions and experiences in a nonjudgmental setting. Occasionally someone would show signs of serious problems, and I was called in to counsel the person or to resolve a theological disagreement, of which there were many. Frequently a few colorful characters would try to dominate the discussions or make "off the wall" comments. For example, one evening, one of the questions asked was, "Who is the person you most admire as a role model?" A man who evidently had ties to a neo-Nazi group replied, "Adolf Hitler!" That was definitely not a situation where one could simply respond, "Thank you for sharing." But it became a teachable moment about the incompatibility of racism or any other kind of bigotry with Christianity or any other civilized religion.

The volunteers loved these sessions and often remarked that they got much more out of them than they were able to contribute. As Patrick observed, "Isn't it ironic that we had to visit a prison in order to participate in a faith-sharing group? In all my years of being involved in parish activities, I have never experienced anything like this in any outside parish."

We ended the session at 8:30 p.m. by forming a large circle around the chapel with everyone holding hands. After a period of shared petitions, during which we prayed for anyone having problems or going to the parole board or for sick loved ones, we then ended by praying together the Lord's Prayer, the Hail Mary, and the Glory Be before we went our separate ways—the volunteers and I to our homes, and the prisoners back to their cells.

FINDING TRUSTWORTHY CHAPEL WORKERS

Finding chapel workers was a slow and painful learning process. George was too old to do much physical work. His sole responsibility had been to type a list of who would be allowed to attend our Wednesday evening mass and Bible study and also an occasional memo. His desk was in my office, which meant he had to leave whenever I wanted to counsel someone. I quickly resolved the problem by counseling people in the sacristy of the chapel, where I would be near enough to supervise the workers in the chapel. George could type his memos in the chapel library adjoining the other side of the sanctuary, giving us the privacy we needed.

Soon after I arrived, George developed prostate cancer. Because he was left incontinent after the surgery, he decided to retire from his position in the chapel and was able to get a clerk position in his unit, which was on the opposite end of the prison. That way he would not have to worry about having an accident while away from his cell. I threw a little retirement party for him to honor him for his many years of faithful service to the chapel. I also breathed a silent prayer that I would find someone compatible with my vision of what needed to be done, particularly someone capable of doing some physical labor to fix up the chapel.

Some of my early choices weren't very good. One man fell in love with one of my volunteers, a married woman whose husband was outraged to find a love letter from him. One was a member of a gang who had convinced me he could make money for the chapel by selling greeting cards in the cellblocks. The common currency in prison was packs of cigarettes, so he soon acquired a large supply of packs, which then mysteriously disappeared before they could be exchanged for coffee, creamer, and cookies for Bible study, as he had promised.

I soon discovered I had to learn how to say no as well as to develop an essential sixth sense to prevent certain con artists from taking advantage of me. One of the most disastrous events occurred only a year after my arrival. I had grown suspicious of some shady activities among my new chapel workers. I ordered office and housekeeping supplies rather sparingly from the facility warehouse once a month, only as needed. Suddenly, huge shipments of unordered supplies began appearing on a regular basis and then disappearing just as mysteriously. I heard through the prison grapevine that my workers had bribed a fellow prisoner who worked in the warehouse to sneak the extra items into the order, which they then sold in the cell blocks to other prisoners.

One of the additional supplies that caught my attention was a full carton of latex gloves.

"Where did these come from?" I inquired of my newly hired clerk, Butch.

"They probably made a mistake in the warehouse," he said, "but don't send them back. You never know when they might come in handy." By then I was aware that latex gloves are frequently used in prison in place of condoms, so I was not convinced that the appearance of a whole carton of them was a mistake.

I asked the sister who had gotten me involved in the AIDS Unit years earlier what to do about it. She was adamant that it was all my imagination and refused to believe that there was a problem. She even went so far as to say, "In all my years of being a prison chaplain, no prisoner ever lied to me!" But she was only at Sing Sing one day a week, working at another prison for the remainder of the week, and the men at Sing Sing were always on their best behavior around her. They told her only what she wanted to hear, some of them displaying signs of great piety in her presence but behaving like the devil in her absence.

Meanwhile, Tony warned me, "Father, those guys have quite a racket going on, and everybody knows about it. This could cost you your job if you don't put a stop to it."

I had always trusted the sister's advice in the past, but she was no help now. The problem was serious and getting worse, so in desperation I asked my supervisor, the assistant deputy superintendent, what to do. His response was immediate. He fired all the workers. Their cells were searched, but nothing incriminating was found. They even had to endure degrading strip searches of their bodily cavities. None of this uncovered the true nature of the problem. I knew from then on that I could never trust the administration to use common sense in coping with problems. They became the very last people I would ever turn to for help. Unfortunately, it was also the end of what had been a wonderful relationship with the sister, who blamed me for persecuting the chapel workers. Although she continued to come in one day a week to visit the AIDS patients, her subsequent contact with me was rare and distant.

Those workers were followed by several other problem makers, including one who was involved in smuggling weapons into the facility. I had presumed that since Rudy lived in the Honor Block he would be a good choice. Thus I was horrified when the DSS (deputy superintendent of security) called me into his office to show me the weapons and explain how they were smuggled into the facility.

"Your chapel clerk's cell is right next to a mobster's cell," he explained. "The mobster's mother has a canning machine. Look at these Campbell's soup cans. That sweet old lady packed switch blades in them and then brought them to her son in a care package on a visit. He didn't want to get caught, so he bribed your worker to keep them in his cell. During a random cell search the officer noticed that the cans were too heavy and rattled when he shook them, so your clerk got busted and was sent to the Box [the name commonly used for solitary confinement]."

I was outraged about what Rudy had done, even more so when I visited him in the Box. "But Father Ron," he pleaded, "I didn't know anything about it. Jack [the mobster] just asked me to do him a favor and hold a few things for him because he had too much in his cell before our inspection. Please, Father, talk to the deputy superintendent and get him to go easy on me."

His plea fell on deaf ears. The sight of those weapons that he had helped smuggle into the facility had destroyed any sense of compassion I might otherwise have felt for him.

Several others I had tried to take on as chapel workers were involved with drugs. I received a large supply of rosaries from an outside source, each one packaged in a small plastic bag. A new worker named Max had recently transferred from another facility where he had been a chapel clerk and had been highly recommended by his former chaplain. Max was a delightful fellow, but I began to notice that some strange individuals who never came to mass were dropping by the chapel during the week to talk to him. This was unusual, since the chapel officer in charge was very strict about not allowing people to come to the chapel without authorization. One day I discovered all of the rosaries had been removed from the plastic bags they came in.

"Max," I asked, "what happened to the bags the rosaries were in?"

"Oh, I thought I'd clean up around here and throw them away. Nobody needs those little plastic bags," he replied.

"But," I protested, "those bags were there for a purpose. When I keep a bunch of rosaries in my pocket to distribute in the Box they get all tangled up if they aren't in separate bags."

Shortly afterward I received an anonymous letter from one of our chapel members:

Please, Father Ron,

There are big sins committed in the House of God by this new clerk Max. We are all talking about it. He is dealing drugs in the House of God. That is why all those junkies are hanging out in the chapel. He uses those little plastic bags from the rosaries for the drugs. Please, Father, you must do something about this immediately before it goes to the superintendent! We have a good thing going for us in this chapel, and we don't want it ruined. That's why we came to you first. Please take care of this now!

Thank you!

From all of us Christians

I called the chaplain in the prison where Max had been before coming to Sing Sing and told him about it. He adamantly protested, "I assure you that Max would never do anything like that." I wasn't so sure, but the evidence was definitely not in his favor. I didn't explain why, but I told the chapel officer in charge not to allow Max in the chapel when I wasn't there. Max got the hint and requested a job transfer. The weird characters immediately stopped dropping by the chapel. Shortly afterward, much to my relief, Max was transferred to another prison.

Those early years were very trying, but they provided an invaluable education, and gradually I grew in my ability to cope with some truly fascinating characters. At times, some of the men would pull me aside and warn me about certain suspicious individuals who were taking advantage of me. Sometimes I would listen; other times I had to learn the hard way. But the example of the forgiving father in the gospel story of the prodigal son continually inspired me to keep on trying to believe in people, even when everyone else had given up on them.

Most of the men, however, preferred to follow the example of the "older brother" in the story. They were not too inclined to forgive or to give anyone a second chance. I could understand where they were coming from. As Tony explained, "I don't want to be an enabler or to give the impression that I condone negative behavior."

"But," I replied, "all of you have engaged in various forms of negative activity at various times in your lives. Sometimes people just need someone to believe in their ability to do better. That is why I'm here."

I always believed that the vast majority of the people with whom I worked were sincerely trying to do the right thing. Many were damaged in numerous ways by the problems of life, but working with them to help them rebuild their lives was by far the most fulfilling experience of my life.

FINDING SOME BETTER CHAPEL WORKERS

John

One of the first good clerks I hired was John, a recent graduate from the New York Theological Seminary's (NYTS) master's degree program at Sing Sing. This seminary, originally under the leadership of the late Dr. Bill Webber, has offered a master's degree in professional studies at Sing Sing since 1982, providing a wonderful opportunity for fifteen carefully selected men from prisons all over the state to come to Sing Sing for one year of studies. John was a student in the program when I first arrived, and I was immediately impressed by him. He was never a drug addict and was an unlikely person to find in a maximum-security prison. He told me, "I was engaged to be married. Life was great until the day I came home from work unexpectedly and found my fiancée in bed with another man. At that point, I freaked out and killed them both. I also shot myself, but I survived. While I was recovering in the hospital, I received a letter from my fiancée's sister. At first I was afraid to open it, but when I did I couldn't believe what I read. She told me she understood and that she forgave me."

All those years later John still choked up while describing the impact of that letter. "Her message of forgiveness changed my life. I am at peace now and am trying to use my prison time to be of service to others." He got the job and turned out to be a fine clerk with lots of innovative ideas. John was working for me when I got permission to bring in a computer for the office. Previously, all work had been done on an ancient manual typewriter. Although he had never used a computer before, since very few of the other offices where prisoners worked allowed them access to a computer, John quickly mastered it and was able to simplify many office tasks that previously had been done by hand. Callout lists of names and locations of men allowed to attend Bible study had taken George most of the week to laboriously type but could now be stored on the computer and printed in seconds.

Alejandro

After John came Alejandro, an Army veteran from the Gulf War. Like John, he was a graduate of the NYTS master's program and had never been a drug addict. He was a very clean-cut, military-looking young man with a delightful sense of humor. At our interview

Alejandro informed me: "Although I never actually killed anyone myself, I was with a group of friends when someone was killed. Not wanting to rat anybody out, I ended up being convicted of felony murder and received a life sentence."

Alejandro was an outstanding clerk and was also bilingual, a tremendous help in working with our numerous Hispanic parishioners, translating all of my Bible study worksheets into Spanish. In addition, he learned to play the bass guitar, which was a great boost to our instrumental group, freeing my left hand from having to play the bass line to add descants and other interesting musical effects.

Rob

Another outstanding clerk was Rob, also a graduate of NYTS. His grammar was impeccable, and he had an incredible vocabulary. All I had to do was tell him to write a memo or letter to someone about a particular topic, and he would immediately create a flawless masterpiece. He was more competent than any parish secretary I ever had. Even better, although Rob had been a long-term drug addict, he had long since changed his ways and was constantly trying to help others to get clean. His presence in the chapel and the life he was leading in prison spoke far more eloquently than anything I could ever say about the power of God's grace to overcome addiction.

Stu

It is difficult to find adequate words to describe my trusted worker and companion Stu, who worked for me from 1998 until my departure from Sing Sing in 2011. Stu was a Vietnam veteran, a combat photographer who had seen it all. Many of his photos were featured in the Army's *Stars and Stripes* newspaper. "I used to go up in the helicopter with POWs and their interrogators. If no one answered

their questions, they would start throwing people out of the helicopter until someone gave them the information they wanted."

In the chapel Stu saw a long string of workers come and go, and
he outlasted all of them. I never had to worry about him doing
drugs, selling drugs, fighting, or doing any other illicit activities.
He would not tolerate anyone else defiling our little place of refuge either. He was my chief liturgical "decorator," always keeping
the altar looking spectacular. During the season of Ordinary Time,
the altar, the backdrop behind the crucifix, the tables, and the
music stand were all draped in beautifully tailored green cloths.
That changed to purple for Advent and Lent, white and gold for
Christmas and Easter, and bright red for Palm Sunday and Pente-
cost. No matter what time of the year it was, the chapel always
looked magnificent. In addition, he took over the stained-glass
window restoration project (described in Chapter 7) after his
predecessor died of cancer.

Stu was a devout Catholic who faithfully prayed the Divine
Mercy chaplet every day at 3 p.m. and fasted on bread and water
twice a week. He had a fundamentalist attitude toward the scriptures and was eagerly looking forward to the end of the world,
when all of his enemies would be thrown into hell. We clashed on
theological issues all the time, but he was my right-hand man in the
chapel. It was a travesty of justice that had put him in prison. He
was convicted in the local newspaper of killing his wife long before
he went to trial. To this day he maintains his innocence, and from
reading the transcript of his trial I believe him. So does his trial attorney. Contrary to popular belief, not everyone in prison claims
to be innocent. I have heard people confess to far more crimes than
the ones of which they were convicted. But there are numerous
miscarriages of justice. Some of the wrongly convicted are eventually exonerated, but usually not until after twenty or more years.
After the best years of their lives have been taken away from them,

a trite "sorry for the inconvenience" only reflects how dysfunctional our criminal justice system is.

I discuss our chapel retreats in depth later, but this excerpt from the closing talk at one retreat is appropriate here.

"Francis, Rebuild My Church"

When Saint Francis was praying in the ancient ruins of the long abandoned Chapel of San Damiano, he heard Jesus speak to him from the crucifix: "Francis, rebuild my church." Saint Francis saw the rubble all around him and thought the Lord wanted him to repair the badly damaged chapel. So, with the help of some friends, Francis fixed the place up. Eventually, however, he learned that the Lord was concerned about something much greater than the physical structure of that little chapel. The church consists of God's people, many of whom are broken and disillusioned. Saint Francis discovered that rebuilding the church involves rebuilding the community of God's people.

That is what has been happening here in the church of Sing Sing. Upon my arrival here, the physical shape of the chapel was a mess. But even worse, it was empty. There were only a handful of people coming. There was no music. It was a depressing place to visit. The members were like scattered stones, with no one to build them into a church.

However, there were six men in a Bible study group led by a fellow prisoner named Tony. The group had been meeting once a week for two years to pray for God to renew the Catholic chapel. They were the first builders of this community. Various leaders have come and gone, all of whom have left their mark on our community. Some of them shared their artistic talents to restore beauty to this once drab place. Others shared their elbow grease to clean up many years' accumulation of dirt and grime. Others were like modern-day versions of the apostle Paul, whose greatest missionary work was done while in prison. They went back to the blocks and invited their friends to become a part of this wonderful community.

4

Ministry of Hospitality

Mark arrived at Sing Sing in 2003. I first met him when he asked me about the possibility of seeing his grandmother in the hospital before she died. I helped him get the necessary documents to prove she was his biological grandmother so he could make a deathbed visit in accordance with departmental regulations, and we began to get acquainted. This young man had a delightful personality. He was the kind of person who would be the life of any party. So I gave him my usual icebreaker question, "How did such a nice guy like you ever end up in here?"

Mark explained: "Two of my uncles were killed in the World Trade Center. This left our whole family devastated. I had gotten a serious shoulder injury at my job in a warehouse shortly before 9/11. The pain was so bad and so constant that I got addicted to prescription painkillers. Once I realized I was hooked, I tried to get into a drug rehab, but my lousy insurance wouldn't pay for it. I couldn't afford to pay for it myself, so I tried to get help from Social Services. They told me that because I was working I was earning too much money to get any assistance from them. Meanwhile, my whole family was sliding into a depression over the death of my uncles, and I eventually resorted to illegal drugs, which were much more readily available than the prescribed painkillers. After a while, my habit got so bad that I resorted to robbing convenience stores to get the money needed to support my growing heroin habit. That's how I ended up here."

I was so impressed by Mark and his eagerness to help around the chapel that I asked him if he would like to be one of my chapel workers. When he asked me what I wanted him to do, I told him that with his outgoing personality he could reach out to people who don't come to church and invite them. In addition, every Sunday when people gathered for mass, he could approach any of the constant stream of newcomers and make them feel at ease, urging them to sign up for our various activities. "Let's call your role here a ministry of hospitality," I suggested.

"That sounds to me like serving tea and crumpets."

"Well," I explained, "serving coffee and cookies after mass will be part of your job description, so you aren't too far off."

"What's the big deal about hospitality? It seems like we are bribing people to come to mass by offering coffee and cookies," Mark said.

"When you go fishing, you have to use the right bait. If a cup of coffee and a cookie will get people in the door, they might learn something that could help to change their lives. Enticing people to come in is part of the process, which is why your job is so important, not only in here, but out in the yard as well. People know you work for me. They will be much more likely to approach you with a concern or to voice a complaint than to approach me directly. Every time you go to the yard, think of yourself as going fishing."

Mark took his job seriously and quickly began reeling in all kinds of fish. He would go out to the recreational yard in B Block, where he and most of the other newcomers lived, and engage others in conversations that eventually would lead to an invitation to come to church.

The yard is a big open space where everybody hangs out together. Many different groups congregate there, the white guys at one table, the Jamaicans, Latin Kings, Muslims, Rat Hunters, Ñetas, and Bloods each at their own separate picnic table. Most of the time they get along, but they have to respect one another's space. No one can join a table without being personally invited. While proselytizing is not allowed, with Mark's outgoing personality he was able to socialize with practically anybody, and since they all knew he worked for me, religion was often a topic of conversation.

Very often, people would have all kinds of reasons why they didn't like church. "They are all a bunch of hypocrites," or "priests are all child molesters," or "I was thrown out of Catholic school when I was a kid and hell will freeze over before I ever go back to church." Mark had the kind of personality that overcame their objections and convinced them to come and see for themselves what our chapel was like.

One of the biggest objections Mark encountered was, "I heard that that priest allows child molesters to come to mass, and I don't want to be around any tree jumpers."

"So you think your shit doesn't stink?" Mark said. "When people were ready to stone a woman for adultery, Jesus told them to 'let the one who is without sin cast the first stone.' Molesting a child is a terrible crime, and I would go ballistic if any tree jumper ever did that to my kid, but do you really think that murder is any better? If you have kids, would you rather have them dead or molested? No crime is good. That's why we're all here. But if we start eliminating all of the sinners from the chapel, we will end up with an empty chapel. The reason we have prison chaplains is to help us become better people. If you think you are already so saintly, you belong in heaven instead of Sing Sing. If you want to become a better person, try coming to the chapel."

Mark's persuasive tactics worked on some but made him extremely unpopular with others, because he was challenging the whole criminal value system known as the prison code. That was taboo and often resulted in some serious clashes, particularly with the old-timers, who were appalled by his attitude. Nevertheless, chapel attendance increased drastically due to his persistence.

Mark prepared a popular quarterly newsletter that described our various chapel activities. We sent it to every person listed as Catholic on the prison census. Many of the men never received any mail at all, so getting a letter from the chaplain, even a form letter, letting them know what we do in the chapel and that they were welcome to join us, meant a lot and brought in more newcomers.

One of the biggest obstacles to hospitality in the chapel was the elite group of "holier than thous" who looked with great disdain upon people with ongoing drug problems. They did their best to make such "sub-standard Christians" feel unwelcome, accusing them of hypocrisy because of their failure to stay clean. One of Mark's favorite lines in dealing with them was: "I guess you don't need to come to church. You are already so holy you have your place in heaven reserved. So why don't you make room here for all of us sinners who are still trying to grow in our faith?"

About this time I became involved in helping someone I had never met get out of prison. Glenn Harris, one of the new men in the chapel, told me about Martin Tankleff, who had been convicted of killing his parents during his senior year of high school. "I know he didn't do it," Glenn said, "because I drove the getaway car for the guy who killed them."

"Then you have a moral obligation to speak up so that innocent man can go home."

"I know that," Glenn said, "but I am afraid of the consequences."

"What do you mean by that?"

"People will think I am a snitch and try to kill me. I don't know what to do."

Not only did someone threaten to kill him, for which he ended up in protective custody, but he later told me that someone from the Suffolk County District Attorney's Office came to Sing Sing to threaten that if he testified on behalf of Tankleff they would make sure he spent the rest of his life in prison.

Glenn was released shortly afterward and came to stay in my halfway house. He was a bundle of nerves. He was unable to sleep and had broken out in hives. He was, however, able to do an interview with Erin Moriarty from the CBS News program *48 Hours* and told the whole story.

He was quickly arrested on a parole violation and went to the Suffolk County Jail. While he was in the jail, one of the other prisoners threatened him, "I know where your kids live, and if you open your mouth they will fuckin' disappear."

Glenn was terrified. He really wanted to do the right thing, but he could not risk sacrificing his children. He did, however, sign a written affidavit authorizing me to testify about what he had told me. So, when he subsequently got cold feet at the court hearing, Tankleff's attorney asked me to testify on Glenn's behalf.

This was highly publicized in the newspapers and on television and created quite a controversy within the prison population. While some were happy to hear that I was trying to help an innocent man be freed, those who didn't know the whole story were upset, not only about Glenn being a snitch, but because they thought I was, too. Since Mark served as my representative in the yard, they addressed their concerns to him.

"Father Ron is a rat because he testified against someone in court to get him into trouble."

Mark defended me. "Father Ron never testified against anyone either in or out of the fuckin' court. He never accused anybody of a damned thing, and nobody has been arrested. He is only trying to help an innocent man go free after being unjustly imprisoned for seventeen years for a crime he didn't commit. What the hell is wrong with that?"

Without Mark's strong defense, a lot of guys would have boy-cotted the chapel. But once they understood what was really going on, they began to follow the case with great excitement and were overjoyed when Tankleff finally was set free in 2007. The real killers were never brought to justice, but at least Tankleff is a free man who has since graduated from law school so he can help others.

The most important part of prison ministry is not what the priest does, but what the people do. My job was simply to call them to action and provide some guidance along the way. They were the ones who shared their faith in the yard and in the cell blocks, pri-marily by the way they lived and interacted with the people around them. They were the ones who got people to come to church and consider giving God a try. I continually reminded them that Saint Francis said, "Preach always, and *occasionally* use words." How the chapel members behaved on a daily basis was far more powerful than anything I could say in a homily at mass.

After his baptism Ricky, one of our choir members, came to me with the words to a song he had just written, reminding me, "You always tell us that we have far more opportunities than you do to spread the gospel back in the cell blocks, so I wrote this song that was inspired by Jesus's calling of the disciples to be fishers of men."

It was a call to action, which I set to music in the form of a marching song, which we were able to sing when Cardinal Dolan celebrated mass in our chapel.

5

Holy Week

Remembering the disappointing Christmas attendance, by February I had already begun to encourage people to participate in our upcoming Holy Week services. Holy Week has always been the highlight of the year for me, and I had put my heart and soul into the preparations in every parish where I had been assigned, both as a priest and earlier as a parish music director. My first Holy Week at Sing Sing was no exception. Our little choir practiced diligently to learn new music for all of the liturgies. It would never rival the Cadet Choir at West Point, but everybody had fun. We had special rites of initiation for Brandy and Tex, who were preparing for confirmation, and every Sunday I encouraged the congregation to come to our services for Holy Thursday, Good Friday, and the Easter Vigil.

On Holy Thursday the superintendent informed the chaplains, "The commissioner of corrections has mandated that all chaplains throughout the state conduct a special interfaith prayer service to commemorate the anniversary of the assassination of Martin Luther King tomorrow."

I couldn't believe it. "Doesn't the commissioner realize that tomorrow is Good Friday? I have my hands full preparing for our own commemoration of the assassination of Jesus Christ!"

But the superintendent insisted, "I am just relaying orders from on high, and we must follow them."

We managed to throw together a simple interfaith service that we could do on Friday morning so it wouldn't interfere with the services in the Protestant or Catholic chapels in the afternoon or the Jewish Passover seder in the evening, but I was quite irate that we were expected to drop everything at the last minute to accommodate this eleventh-hour mandate from Albany. I would eventually discover that such directives were commonplace and to be expected, regardless of what else was going on.

Meanwhile, after all of the months of preparation, the officers in B Block, from which most of my parishioners came, decided to ignore the memo authorizing the men to attend our Holy Thursday evening service, so only a few were there. I was furious and complained to the DSP, who assured me it would be taken care of for the remaining services.

We had the service for Martin Luther King on Friday morning, and the auditorium was filled to capacity. Even though a memo had been distributed to all of the housing blocks authorizing them to come that afternoon for our Good Friday service, once again most of the congregation was prevented from attending. By the end of the service the Exec Team had already gone home, so there was no way of getting anyone to do anything about it, which is why the same thing happened for the Saturday evening Easter Vigil. Our volunteers came in, and most of the choir was able to get there. I had been given special authorization by the bishop to confirm Brandy and Tex, but there were very few people in the congregation.

Brandy was from B Block, where most of those who had been prevented from coming to the Easter Vigil were from, so I asked him what happened. "The officer on my gallery knew I was going to be confirmed, and he made sure I got over here. But the memo authorizing everyone else to come was thrown out, so the guard at the gate wouldn't allow anyone else to come."

On the day after Easter I wrote a blistering letter to the superintendent, letting him know I had bent over backward to accommodate the commissioner's mandated service, but that nobody had cooperated with me to allow my parishioners to commemorate the holiest week of the year for all Christians. The superintendent was a Catholic and should have been as upset as I was, but he was more dismayed that I was angry about his incompetent officers refusing to do their job. This was the disheartening beginning of my celebrations of Holy Week in Sing Sing.

Over the years our celebration of Holy Week evolved considerably. Our congregation soon doubled and then tripled in size, and the guards became more accustomed to seeing the men come to the chapel almost every night of the week. I also eventually developed a rapport with certain key administration officials who helped make things happen. But I had to combat incompetent and bigoted officers who repeatedly refused to honor any form of Catholic activity, even though they bent over backward to accommodate the needs of Muslims, Five Percenters, Rastafarians, Protestants, Jews, and even Wiccans. So I made copies of the memo authorizing the men to come to the chapel and distributed a copy to everyone who came the previous Sunday. That shouldn't have been necessary, but it made a huge difference.

EDUCATING THE PARISHIONERS
ABOUT HOLY WEEK

There was a constant turnover of the prison population, which meant that every year we had many members who had never experienced a Holy Week liturgy. To help them better appreciate its meaning, I showed movies like *Jesus of Nazareth* and *The Passion of the Christ* in the chapel during Lent. The entire prison population watched *The Passion of the Christ* in the auditorium when it first came out. I sat there with them and was amazed at the impact it had.

Danny, a young man with a long history of drug abuse and from a typically dysfunctional family with no religious background, sat there mesmerized. Normally during films people would sit in the auditorium with their friends and chitchat. Some made out sexually. Others smoked reefers. But on this occasion there was absolute silence. At the end of the film some of the men walked out of the auditorium with tears streaming down their face, which was unthinkable in the prison culture.

The next day Danny told me: "In the past, holidays of whatever sort, Christmas, Easter, or the Fourth of July, were just an excuse to party and go on a long binge. I had no idea what any of those holidays meant. This is the first time I ever saw what actually happened to Jesus."

There was the same reaction every succeeding year when I showed this film in the chapel. Many of the men had never even heard of Holy Week and were spellbound to see how Jesus had been brutalized and crucified by the Roman soldiers, whom they immediately compared to some of their own prison guards.

Understanding the full meaning of Holy Week inspired the men. Our faithful choir members, along with our outstanding group of instrumentalists, worked for two months to learn all the music. Some of the singers were somewhat musically impaired, with raspy voices after many years of heavy smoking and drug abuse, but the excitement built as they worked together to prepare for something that they began to sense was very special.

Lent is traditionally the time for preparing new converts for receiving the sacraments of initiation—baptism, confirmation, and

Eucharist. Part of that preparation involves celebrating the rites of welcoming, election, and scrutinies with the prospective converts and their sponsors. These are very moving rituals and are done in front of the whole congregation. The converts kneel in front of the altar, and their sponsors lay their hands on them at Sunday mass throughout the season of Lent. All of these activities led to a gradual increase in excitement and anticipation within the whole congregation. We went over each of the Holy Week liturgies in our weekly class so everyone would understand the significance of what was about to happen. The lectors rehearsed their assigned readings in front of the class, which critiqued the readers until they learned to deliver the words flawlessly with proper diction. This was quite a challenge for some of them, who had spoken street slang all their lives. The altar servers rehearsed like the Bolshoi Ballet to coordinate their movements.

The altar decor was elevated to the extravagant during Holy Week. On Palm Sunday the altar and backdrop of the large crucifix were ablaze in red with festoons of palm branches all over the sanctuary. Like all Catholics, everyone was familiar with Palm Sunday as the day when palms are distributed. As in many outside parishes, there were plenty of "A & P Catholics" in Sing Sing who came to church only to get ashes on Ash Wednesday and palms on Palm Sunday, with no idea of the context of those rituals. But I looked at it as an opportunity to clarify the meaning of our faith. Once the men appeared in the chapel, regardless of what was motivating them to come, I was able to explain what Holy Week was all about and then encourage them to come back for the rest of it.

We changed the altar decor back to Lenten purple for our Wednesday evening mass, and the next day we switched everything to white for Holy Thursday. We constructed an altar of repose, a pedestal decorated with fabric, lace, silk flowers, and candles, overhung with a cloth canopy, in the rear corner. Stu turned into a phenomenal fashion designer in the way he coordinated all of the changes of decor.

"You never knew that coming to prison would turn you into an interior decorator," I teased him.

"Oh, if only my buddies from Vietnam could see me now!"

HOLY THURSDAY

In the prison setting the foot washing was especially memorable. I encouraged all of the men to participate, not just the traditional twelve to represent the twelve apostles. For people who were accustomed to being harassed, abused, and humiliated every day by prison staff to have their feet washed and kissed by their priest was an incredibly moving and memorable experience.

Since almost everyone in the chapel had their feet washed, this portion of the liturgy took a considerable amount of time. Many of the men had serious attention deficit problems, but never once did the atmosphere deteriorate into a circus environment with people talking and laughing. They looked on in wonder and amazement in total silence. I had celebrated this ritual in every parish where I had been assigned, but never had a ritual had such a profound impact on the congregation.

"I have seen people get their feet washed before, but it always seemed like an archaic custom that meant nothing to me," Tony said. "But seeing a priest kiss the feet of convicted criminals totally blew me away."

The reaction of the congregation, in turn, affected me. While I was kneeling in front of those men, washing, drying, and kissing their feet, it didn't matter that some of those feet needed a much better scrubbing than I could give them and that some were infected with all kinds of fungi. During that sacred moment within the liturgy I became Jesus washing the feet of his disciples, but simultaneously I also was conscious that I was washing the feet of almighty God, who was present in every single one of those poor rejects from society. This was the highlight of my year and made an impression on me that I will never forget.

At the end of the mass the entire congregation processed to the altar of repose, which, I explained, represented the Garden of Gethsemane, and everybody gathered around to pray in silence for the rest of the evening. I have never seen such reverence in any other church setting. For that brief time they were no longer in prison. They were right beside Jesus praying in the Garden, and they did so far more faithfully than the original apostles, who fell asleep.

GOOD FRIDAY

The next morning we stripped all of the decor from the night before, leaving the sanctuary totally bare. We removed the almost life-size crucifix from the wall, draped it in red, and hid it outside the chapel. We then covered the statues with fitted "shrouds" that had been made by Franco with the leftover bolt of white cloth he had used to make robes for the altar servers. Franco had studied fashion design in Italy and had owned his own fashion house in Manhattan before coming to prison.

For the reading of the passion, instead of utilizing the customary three readers for the roles of Jesus, speaker, and narrator, we divided the speaker's role into distinct characters to portray Pontius Pilate, Simon Peter, and the bystander, not only to make it more dramatic, but also to involve more people. Franco, with his bald head and thick Sicilian accent, dressed in a white altar-server's robe, had the role of Pontius Pilate, the Roman procurator, which made it a most memorable production.

For the veneration of the cross the altar servers carried our huge crucifix into the chapel and unveiled it. After hearing what the cross represents in their own lives, the men came up to venerate it with great fervor and devotion. At the end of the liturgy the altar servers carried the crucifix in procession throughout the chapel in profound silence.

HOLY SATURDAY

We spent all day Saturday preparing for the Easter Vigil that would take place that evening. Everything that had been removed for Good Friday had to be returned. First, we uncovered the statues and decorated the whole chapel with silk flowers and colorful cloth hangings. The highlight of the vigil was the baptism of our class of catechumens. Every year for the occasion we borrowed the baptismal tank from the Protestants so we could baptize by full immersion. Unfortunately, the only faucet near enough for the hose to reach the tank had only cold water. Stu loved it. "This will separate the true Catholics from the phonies," he teased. "This is how we test their faith and fortitude."

Tony protested, "If that's the case, why don't we fill the tank with ice cubes?" We compromised and filled the tank the night before in the hope that the water would reach room temperature by the next day. On Saturday afternoon the men carried up some buckets of hot water from the basement. Even so, it was a chilling experience when our converts stepped into that tank.

That evening, just before we began the vigil, I informed the men that they needed to use their imagination. "Instead of being locked up inside of prison," I explained, "we must imagine ourselves outside, gathered around a large bonfire, where we are going to tell some stories about the origins of our faith."

Then we lit our "bonfire," which was a wad of cotton balls soaked with rubbing alcohol in a metal pot. From that fire we lit the paschal candle, which represented the resurrected Christ. And from that candle everyone in the congregation was able to light his own taper as we processed down the center aisle.

The baptisms took place in the middle of the liturgy and made a profound impression on the whole congregation, most of whom had never seen a baptism by immersion before. But the cold water made an even more profound impression on the men who were baptized. One young man, Jerry, who had some serious mental problems, shouted, "This is *cold*," as he climbed into the baptismal tank. Another one, Dave, got in before I had blessed the water, so he stood there shivering with teeth chattering through the very long blessing before being baptized.

After their baptism they went into a side room (our chapel library) to dry off and change clothes while the rest of the congregation renewed their baptismal vows and blessed themselves from the newly blessed holy water in the baptismal font. Then we led the newly baptized, dressed in white altar-server robes, in procession down the center aisle for their confirmation as we sang *Amazing Grace*. This was the liturgical highlight of the year, and we celebrated accordingly with a huge cake with cannoli filling from the locally famous Homestyle Desserts Bakery in Peekskill, one of the best bakeries in the Hudson Valley. It was difficult to squeeze the Easter Vigil liturgy with baptisms and confirmations into the two hours allotted to us, so we sometimes had to speed things up a bit toward the end to make sure there was enough time for cake and coffee. We had a lot of ragged edges in our celebration, but it was exciting, and everybody knew that Jesus Christ had truly risen.

6

Celebrating Christmas
behind Bars

My first Christmas at Sing Sing had taught me how painful it was for prisoners to celebrate such a joyful holiday behind bars. Memories of all of the good times they used to have only added to their depression. To cope with the pain, many would stay in their cell all day and try to pretend it wasn't Christmas. Those who had formerly gotten drunk or high on holidays would frequently try to do the same while in prison. Suicidal thoughts were common. I posted a letter to the congregation on the bulletin board in the chapel throughout the Christmas season to let the men know that I recognized what a painful, depressing time this was for many of them and that I would always be available to anyone who needed to talk. They all knew that anything they told me was confidential, and many spoke freely about their suicidal feelings. Any other staff member would have been required to report such a conversation to the Psych Unit, after which the prisoner would have been put in a strip cell with nothing to wear but a paper gown. Because I was a priest, I was the only person in the prison not legally required to do so. However, I took those conversations very seriously, sometimes spending hours with a person to convince him that life was worth living. That was not easy.

Vinnie, for example, was a child molester who hated himself and had tried to kill himself on numerous occasions, with slash marks up and down both arms. "What do I have to look forward to?" he asked. "Everybody hates me. My family wants nothing to do with me. I will be on the sex offender registry on my release. Why should I stay alive?"

I had no solution to Vinnie's overwhelming problems. But I listened as he poured out his heart in my office. He knew that I cared and that he was not alone. That was what gave him the courage to keep on going.

No one in prison is immune to depression, but people's depression became particularly acute at Christmas time. For that reason I never took any time off during the holiday season. During the sixteen years I worked there, not one of the men I counseled committed suicide at Sing Sing. All most of them needed was an opportunity to talk about their feelings without worrying about the consequences.

Throughout the season of Advent I attempted to educate the men about the spiritual significance of the holiday. It was shocking how few people had any idea why we celebrate Christmas. They knew about Santa and Rudolph, the elves, Christmas trees and mistletoe, but very few understood that we were celebrating the birth of our Savior. I also tried to help them realize that Christmas was not just something that happened two thousand years ago. The true meaning of Christmas is about how our Lord Emmanuel is born within our lives today, something we can celebrate regardless of where we are, with or without the trimmings.

CHRISTMAS CARDS

Christmas cards are extremely popular in prison. Those with relatives or acquaintances want to send them cards, not just to greet them, but to remind them that they are still in prison and hope to hear from them, and also possibly to get a gift from them. The facility stopped buying cards a few years after I arrived, so I purchased around a thousand of them every year; numerous others were donated by friends and charitable organizations. Whenever men asked me for Christmas cards, I told them they would have to come to mass to get them, unless they were in the infirmary, PSU, or the Box, where I also distributed them. Attendance was terrific during the Advent season, and since I only gave out two or three cards at a time, the men needed to keep coming back to accumulate a good selection. Meanwhile, they heard my homilies explaining the true meaning of Christmas.

One day I received a phone call from Debra Classen in Ohio, who had read about our prison ministry at Sing Sing and wanted to offer her assistance. She told me a painful story of how her mother had been raped and murdered many years ago. The perpetrators had never been found, but she, after a long struggle, had become a Catholic, forgiven them, and now wanted to do something for prisoners as a means of demonstrating her forgiveness. "I am a professional artist, Father," she said, "and I was wondering if I could make some Christmas cards for the men in your chapel. To me, that would be a tangible sign of the forgiveness that I have given to the unknown assailants who killed my mother." She asked me for an idea of what kind of picture to use on the card.

"How about the theme of the annunciation?" I suggested. "But show the angel Gabriel appearing to a prisoner in his cell." She felt inspired by the idea and came up with a masterpiece, which is the cover of this book. She also made a large reproduction on canvas to hang in the chapel, which she and her husband personally delivered when they came here to speak to the men about the importance of forgiveness. I liked the painting so much she sent me another reproduction of it for me to hang in My Father's House.

DECORATING FOR CHRISTMAS

In most churches the Christmas decorations traditionally don't go up until Christmas Eve, but we used the decorations to combat holiday depression and started decorating on the first Sunday of Advent, adding a little at a time until Christmas. Over the years the progression got faster simply because it brightened people's spirits so much. Stu loved doing the Christmas decorations. He could rival any of the decorators on Fifth Avenue. He strung garlands with lights and bows all around the chapel and hung large wreaths with more garlands around the crucifix. But the pièce de résistance was the Christmas tree.

After a few years of decorating our little Charlie Brown Christmas tree, I got permission to bring in a new one, a nine-foot-tall artificial spruce. We placed it on top of a large table, so it towered over the whole chapel. "How will we ever be able to decorate this enormous tree?" Stu asked in mock horror.

"I don't know, but I'm sure you guys will find a way, so let's go to it," I replied.

With no ladder, they had to stand on top of a bookcase to reach the top. They covered the tree with strings of lights, garlands, and every kind of ornament imaginable, including a bunch of cute stuffed dogs. They also arranged stacks of gift-wrapped empty boxes beneath the tree.

Mark told me about an old man who came into the chapel one day and asked, "Could I just touch the tree? I've been locked up for twenty-five years, and this is the first time I've seen a Christmas tree in prison."

For many years the Protestant chapel was dominated by fundamentalists who considered Christmas trees to be pagan, so we were the only chapel that had a tree, and everybody enjoyed it.

Just before Christmas Eve we placed a beautiful nativity set beneath our altar. When people first came into the chapel during evening services, we had only the Christmas lights on. It was an awesome sight, almost like leaving prison behind and being back home for some, or at least back out on the street. We even left the lights on during the day, and we purposely left the chapel door open so people could see the decorations. Even the Muslims, Jews, and Rastafarians poked their heads in to admire the sight, because it was the only place in the whole prison where people could see something beautiful.

The choir worked especially hard for many weeks to prepare for Christmas. Every year they sang *O Holy Night,* not always on key but always with great enthusiasm. We also had a candlelight procession on Christmas Eve, with the choir carrying real candles down the center aisle while singing *O Come, All Ye Faithful* in English and Spanish. After communion we dimmed the lights and sang *Silent Night* in both languages. Quite a few tears were shed in that dim candlelight.

CHRISTMAS PRESENTS

Although I always stressed that Christmas is not about the decorations and presents, I tried to provide as many of the traditional trimmings as possible to help the men feel loved. Everyone who attended Christmas services got a gift, which usually consisted of a pocket calendar, a candy bar, and some kind of religious holy card, all put together in a small gift-wrapped package with a candy cane on the outside.

Two of our chapel volunteers were from a nearby parish that made sure the men's children received gifts. A couple of months before Christmas I announced at mass that anyone wishing to send Christmas presents to their children should see me. I didn't give any details to the congregation so the ever-present snitches couldn't inform the administration of our plans. Those interested gave me the names, ages, and addresses of their children, which were then relayed to the outside parish. That parish's confirmation class held a series of fundraisers and then went shopping to purchase age-appropriate gifts for all of the children, which they then mailed to their home addresses. The card on the gift indicated that it was from their father. After a few years a local public high school also participated in the project. I never asked the administration for permission to do this project, because I knew that the answer would be no. As many before me have noted, it is much easier to ask for forgiveness after than to get permission. Going by the feedback from the men, the children were thrilled to receive a gift from their father. Here is a thank-you note from one of the men to the parish children who sent the presents:

Dear Friends,

As you can probably imagine, being in prison away from family and friends is difficult and lonely, especially during the Christmas season. This was my fourth Christmas behind bars, and it still is not getting any easier. I miss and love my family so very much, longing each and every day to be with them, holding them in my arms again.

This year, however, through your selfless acts and kind generosity, I know that my two daughters were provided with gifts in my name. It felt as if a small piece of me was there again with them when I closed my eyes and pictured their smiling faces opening the gifts you provided.

Mere words are not possible to express the gratitude and admiration I have for what you have done for both me and my family. You have taken away from your valuable time to truly perform an act of grace for some of the lowliest members of society. We have never met and never will, but you still had a deep-hearted desire to give Christmas joy to my daughters, who were total strangers to you, and that speaks volumes about the type of persons you are. If the world had more people like you in it, more caring, warm-hearted individuals who think of others in a time of need, this would be a much better place indeed. From the bottom of my heart, I thank you.

Sincerely,

Jim

Since approximately half of the congregation was from Latin America where the feast of the Three Kings is the traditional time for gift giving, we had a Three Kings party. Sue, a lovely woman in New Jersey, always sent boxes of deodorant, toothbrushes, shampoo, socks, and other sundries to be used as gifts. But to liven things up a bit, I had the men pick numbers out of a hat, and whatever numbers they drew determined which gifts they would receive. We also had chips, salsa, and soda for refreshments. Little by little the men began looking forward to Christmas each year instead of dreading it. They also began to realize, in many cases for the first time in their lives, the real meaning behind the holiday.

Y2K

The most difficult Christmas for us was the one of 1999. Everybody was worried about the impact of the rollover to the year 2000 (Y2K). There was also talk of riots, so no one was sure what was going to happen.

On Christmas Eve, just before the men were supposed to arrive in the chapel for mass, the chapel OIC poked his head in the chapel to inform me: "Forget about Christmas Eve mass tonight. We have a code blue." A code blue can be called for a variety of reasons, from a miscount of the population to an escape or even as a training exercise, like a fire drill. Sometimes it lasts only an hour or two, or it may last for days. Whenever one occurs, no one knows the cause or how long it will last, but for the duration of the code blue, everyone remains locked in his cell, and all activities are canceled until the problem is resolved.

So, on this occasion, when my parishioners were eagerly looking forward to our Christmas Eve celebration, minutes before they were supposed to be released from their cells, they were informed that nobody could go anywhere. Not yet knowing the cause of the code blue, I went to the watch commander in charge for the evening to see what was going on. He informed me that one of the officers had found some bullets in the prison, and the State Police were called in to investigate.

For the next ten days nobody could leave his cell. That meant no showers or recreation. But it also meant no chapel services for that whole time. As a result, that evening I went cell to cell throughout the facility, calming people down and writing down phone numbers and messages to relay to worried family members. On Christmas morning I celebrated mass in the chapel with a nice young Catholic sergeant as my altar server and sole member of the congregation. I consecrated enough hosts to distribute communion to the rest of my congregation scattered throughout the prison. I hastily reassured them, "We have simply put Christmas on hold until this is over. Whenever you are allowed to return to the chapel, that is when we will celebrate Christmas."

To make matters worse during this stressful time, my mother in the Midwest was in the final stage of cancer and had just entered hospice care at my brother's home in Wisconsin, so I had to fly out there to be with her. But before I left on January 1, I again reassured the men that I would be back to celebrate Christmas with them. Later, it turned out that the bullets had been planted by one of the guards, who was subsequently fired. Coincidentally, something similar happened at the same time in nearby Green Haven Correctional Facility. It seemed that someone wanted a lockdown, whether one was necessary or not. Meanwhile, the unnecessary suffering it caused at a time that was already painful enough was disgusting. But that kind of behavior is sadly a part of the prison system.

7

Chapel Artwork

The chapel had many beautiful artifacts that were obscured by dirt and grime built up over years of neglect. In keeping with our Franciscan theme of rebuilding the church, I began looking for skilled craftsmen to help restore them. That was how I got to know Franco. Sergeant Coop was aware of all the work we were doing in the chapel and suggested that I get to know him, since he lived and worked in 5 Building where she had her office. Besides being a fashion designer, he was a superb craftsman and a fine artist. He had come to Sing Sing on a murder charge long before my arrival but never came to church.

When I stopped in to see him, he greeted me very graciously in typical old-world Italian style and then casually mentioned, "I found a couple of old armchairs that were being discarded, and I was wondering if you would like for me to refinish them for the chapel. If you have a moment, we can go down into the basement so you can take a look at them."

When we arrived in the basement workshop, I was not impressed by what I saw. The chairs looked like junk, which is why they were being discarded. But Franco insisted, "I know how to refinish furniture, and I can make these look like they are brand new."

Since we didn't have any decent-looking chairs in the sanctuary, I told him to go ahead. He refinished the wooden frames and reupholstered them with red vinyl obtained from the Recreational Department. The result was amazing.

When he came to deliver the chairs, he saw our terra cotta Madonna icon, which was falling apart. "What a beautiful Madonna. Would you allow me to repair her?" Since he had done such a masterful job on the chairs, I told him to go ahead. Over the course of the next month he put the broken pieces back together, reinforced everything with chicken wire and many pounds of plaster and then painted it. It was masterfully done, and he was hired. He also came back to church.

Franco put his fashion-designer talents to use in creating altar cloths for our new altar. A carpenter I had originally met when he was in the county jail and who now had his own business in the area built the oak altar with a granite top donated by our volunteers. Once he brought the altar in, I purchased the fabric, one of the Protestant volunteers donated a sewing machine, and Franco made exquisite cloths in each of the liturgical colors—green, purple, white, red, and gold.

STATIONS OF THE CROSS

Franco's next task was to restore the stations of the cross. Through a little research we discovered that they had been made by Jacob Mussner, a German woodcarver who had settled in Val Gardena in Northern Italy in the late nineteenth century. We got in touch with his grandson, who was still running the family business. He estimated that our stations were well over a century old. Now they were covered with a century's worth of dirt and grime, making it difficult to see the scenes they were depicting. Many had fallen on the floor and had broken, and some of the pieces were missing. Each one had to be taken apart, cleaned, and carefully restored. Several of the stations showed a guard with a whip in his hand, but on a couple of them that delicate piece was broken. To replace it, Franco soaked a piece of a tree branch until it was flexible and then molded and notched it to look like a rope whip. It was very tedious work. The project took two years, but it was a labor of love. Since the whole facility knew about the project, it became an opportunity to teach people what the stations represented.

Most of the men were unfamiliar with the stations of the cross. Even Tony, who had been an altar boy and had participated in the stations every Lent during his childhood, admitted, "To me they were just long, boring prayers. I never really paid much attention to them. I knew they were about what happened to Jesus on Good Friday, but it never even occurred to me that they had any relevance to my life today."

"Tony," I reminded him, "you are living the stations of the cross right here in Sing Sing."

"What do you mean?"

"Just wait," I said, "until we introduce them to the Bible study on Wednesday evening, and you will see what I mean."

We used these meditations every Lent to help the men connect their own sufferings in prison with what had happened to Jesus. Here is a sample of one of them:

The Fourteenth Station: Jesus Is Laid in the Tomb
Meditation: Jesus's death *seemed* like a cruel defeat. All he had tried to accomplish *seemed* to have been lost. His whole life's work appeared to be wasted while he lay lifeless in the tomb. But that was not the end! It was the beginning of the victory, which came about in God's time according to God's own plan.

Even when we don't understand what is happening at the moment, or why everything seems to have gone wrong, we must remember that failure and defeat are only temporary illusions within God's overall plan. If we continue to trust and follow him, Jesus will lead us through the "valley of the shadow of death" to the victory of eternal life.

Prayer: Lord Jesus, just as you waited in the prison of the tomb for the fulfillment of God's plan in your life, we wait with you in the tomb of this prison for God to work in our own lives. As we await the Easter dawn of our release, teach us patience, and help us trust that your Father will never abandon or forsake us.

OUR LADY OF HOPE

After Franco had restored the stations of the cross, he turned his attention to two large, unpainted wooden statues and two unpainted wooden pedestals, all of which were in a terrible state of disrepair. I wasn't fond of either of the statues, but George had heard that they were made long ago by one of the prisoners, so I felt it important to preserve them. One was of the Sacred Heart of Jesus. The eyes were always eerily looking straight at you, no matter where you were in the chapel. The other was of Mary holding a crucifix. I had never seen a statue of Mary like that before, so I just assumed it was the product of a prisoner's imagination. For several years the statues had remained untouched, until we got a brochure in the mail about Our Lady of Hope, which is the name of our chapel. The picture in the brochure was of a statue just like ours, except that in the brochure Mary's gown was blue and covered with gold stars.

The brochure told about the apparition that took place in Pontmain, France, on January 17, 1871, during the Franco-Prussian War.

The Prussian Army was rapidly advancing, and the townspeople were frightened and prayed for help. One evening several young children saw a strange formation of stars forming a huge white plume across the sky, and then just above a local house a lovely lady appeared in a blue dress strewn with golden stars. They immediately called for their schoolteacher, Sister Vitaline, to see the beautiful lady, but she couldn't see anything and consequently didn't at first believe them. But then she called for other children to come and look, and without having spoken to the previous children, they described the same lady. As they continued to watch, the children saw a banner unfold in the sky with the words: BUT PRAY MY CHILDREN, GOD WILL SOON ANSWER YOUR PRAYER.

Then a large crucifix appeared that the woman held with both hands. Shortly afterward the vision disappeared. The following day the advancing troops stopped. Ten days later the war ended. All thirty-eight of the soldiers conscripted from Pontmain returned unwounded. After extensive examination the bishop officially recognized the apparition as authentic and named it *Our Lady of Hope*.

Once we realized the significance of the statue, restoring it became our top priority. This was an important symbol of hope for people who were on the verge of despair, not only in nineteenth-century France, but for all of the prisoners in our chapel. The message that God would soon answer their prayer was a much-needed reminder that our Lord cares about all of our problems and is moved by our prayers. This old, broken-down statue suddenly became a wonderful tool for explaining Catholic devotion to Mary, and every stage of its restoration was followed with great enthusiasm by our congregation.

There were two wooden pedestals that originally had held the wooden statues. Like everything else, they were quite an eyesore. We kept them on either side of the doorway to the chapel to hold pamphlets and missalettes. Shortly after my arrival at Sing Sing I had a run-in with the DSP when he started pressuring me to allow the Seventh-Day Adventists to use our chapel. He said the Protestant chapel had so many different groups using it that we ought to allow our chapel to be used for the groups it couldn't accommodate. I knew that if I gave in on this, we would lose control of our chapel and have a whole string of different groups wanting to use it, thus greatly restricting our own use. But he was adamant, so I called the head of ministerial services in Albany as well as our archdiocesan coordinator for prison chaplains and arranged for a meeting. They both backed me and insisted that our chapel had been dedicated as a Catholic chapel and that was how it was intended to be used. Although I had won Round 1, I didn't trust the DSP, so I decided to make the chapel look very "Catholic" by highlighting our statues, knowing that the Seventh-Day Adventists and Pentecostals were particularly opposed to what they considered to be "graven images," which they denounced as idolatry. That was the ulterior motive behind our project to restore our pedestals, enabling us to place the statues on them and give them more prominence. It apparently worked, because we had no more requests to use our chapel.

CRUCIFIX

Our crucifix consisted of a plain, flat wooden cross that had been painted black and an impressive wood carving of a figure of Christ, albeit in terrible condition. Shortly after my arrival Tony tried to clean it up a bit, but it was in such bad shape it needed a major restoration, so this project was put on hold for a few years. Later, Frenchy, who had a background in engineering, designed a new cross that was considerably larger. Whenever we removed the original crucifix for our Good Friday procession, it had to be unbolted, which required the maintenance crew, who then had to come back after the service to bolt it back in place, which was quite a hassle.

The new cross was designed to latch into place without any bolts. It was over six feet long and six inches deep and made a splendid presentation during the Good Friday procession. Unfortunately, the figure of Christ against the new cross appeared to be even more of an eyesore and was so fragile we were afraid it would fall apart. A few years later Chaco, one of our workers, said he could restore it. First, he stripped it down to the bare wood and repaired and strengthened all of the cracked areas with wood putty. Since more than half of the members of the congregation were Hispanic, we decided to stain the wood a deep shade of mahogany, which made it stand out against the oak cross. In addition, Chaco added some long spikes to the crown of thorns and lots of gashes and blood all over the body in the Hispanic tradition, creating a dramatic effect. Unfortunately, Chaco later got into trouble for a drug offense and was transferred out of the facility. For years afterward, whenever Stu changed the fabric backdrop behind the crucifix, he got stuck by those long, sharp thorns, causing him to label the crucifix Chaco's Revenge!

A few years after our chapel renovation began, I ran across a book called *The Convict and the Stained-Glass Windows* by Carmelo Soraci. He had been a prisoner at Sing Sing in the 1940s, shortly after the chapel was built, and with training from the Rambusch Decorating Company had created the beautiful stained-glass windows in both the Catholic and Protestant chapels. These too had greatly deteriorated and needed a lot of work to prevent them from falling apart, so I contacted the family-run company and asked if anyone remembered him. They did and sent Vigo Rambusch to inspect the windows. He then volunteered his son Martin to train my chapel workers how to restore the windows. The company also provided all of the materials for the job. This was a lengthy project, since we had four large windows, plus a rose window above the altar and two smaller windows in the sacristy and library.

Before we were able to get a scaffold, Stu and Smurf, another Vietnam veteran, began working on the lowest panels, which could be removed without a scaffold. When those panels were finished, they stood on top of a bookcase to remove the next row of panels. Then they put a stool on top of the bookcase to remove the next one. Smurf, who looked like a leprechaun, asked, "Are we getting hazardous duty pay for this, Father?"

Stu was balancing on the stool, which was perched precariously on top of the bookcase, and trying to chisel a panel out of the frame. "Father," he called out. "I hope you are praying for me so I don't break my neck."

"Don't worry, Stu, I'll give you last rites if you do."

"THERE IS STILL WORK FOR YOU TO DO"

After Franco was transferred to another facility, Javier took over the leadership of the project. He was an exceptionally fine artist and craftsman from Mexico and worked well with the other workers.

Javier was probably the best soccer player in the prison and was in great demand in the soccer tournaments. He was in excellent physical condition, and he had never smoked or used drugs. He was the picture of health. So, it was unusual when he started complaining about a stomachache. But whenever he went to the infirmary for a checkup, the nurse would give him Pepto-Bismol and tell him to stop complaining. I tried to intervene with the medical director, but he was totally unsympathetic and wouldn't even listen. The nurse administrator was no better. When I spoke with one of the deputy superintendents, he said, "I can't tell the medical people how to do their job and you shouldn't either."

This went on for months, and nobody would help Javier. He began losing weight. He lost the brightness in his eyes, and he was in constant pain. He kept going back to the doctor, who told him to stop complaining. After more than a year the doctor finally approved him for a colonoscopy, which revealed he had stage 3 colon cancer.

Although Javier was confined to our prison infirmary, I got permission to escort him over to the chapel every Sunday morning for mass. This was unheard of, but I think the reason they gave permission was because they knew they were at fault and were afraid of a lawsuit. After mass I was also able to give him a few phone calls to his parents in Mexico. When his brother from Yonkers returned from a visit to their parents, he brought me a large batch of their mother's homemade *mole,* a very savory sauce, in which I cooked some of Javier's favorite foods for him, so it was just like eating his mother's home cooking that he hadn't tasted in many years. (This, of course, was forbidden, so I brought it in as my lunch and managed to smuggle it to him in the hospital.) For a while he actually gained weight from all the extra food, much to the amazement of his doctor, but the disease continued to progress.

Javier had one major goal, which was for his parents to be able to come and visit him before he died. I relayed that to the superintendent, who tried working with the Mexican consulate, but it was totally uncooperative. He, after all, was a prisoner and a poor Indian peasant, not a member of high society. At the very end, when Javier was in the outside hospital and had just been "jump-started" after going into cardiac arrest again, I told him, "Javier, it is OK for you to leave now. Your parents won't be able to come. Jesus is calling you home, and you don't need to worry about anyone else." Within a couple of hours he died, just eleven months after his long-delayed diagnosis.

Javier's death made a huge impact on the chapel community. We had been praying for him for the past year, and he was well loved by everyone. Here is the homily from the funeral mass we had for him:

> Being here in this chapel community bonds us together into a family. As a family, what happens to one affects all of us. We have all journeyed with Javier on his way of the cross this past year. We rejoiced when he made some progress. We shared his frustration during his setbacks. Now, at his death, it's important for us to come together—not only to grieve, but also to celebrate the wonderful life he shared with us. All of us were touched by Javier in different ways, and I'm going to be inviting you to share later what Javier has meant to you. But first, I am going to tell you about a very powerful experience that Javier shared with me recently.
>
> A couple of weeks ago, when Javier had a serious reaction to his chemo treatment, he had a near-death experience. He was out of his body, traveling through a tunnel toward a bright light, and he heard his two brothers who had died in the past few years calling him by name to come and join them. But then he heard another voice saying, "No, not yet. There is still work for you to do." Then he was back in his hospital bed, attached to all kinds of machines.
>
> When I arrived at the hospital a few minutes later, he asked me what kind of work he still needed to do. This was from a man who had just completed the restoration of our stained-glass windows and Saint Joseph's statue. He had also corrected the grammatical errors in my Spanish homilies for the past four years and had even continued to do so every week while he was in the hospital. And he was wondering—what more did God want him to do?
>
> I told him there is only one thing left for him to do—and that was to pray. I told him to pray for his family, especially

his parents, who were still mourning the untimely loss of two of his brothers from accidents. But I also told him to pray for this family here at Sing Sing—for each one of you. And when he was too weak to pray, he could simply offer God his sufferings on behalf of everyone he loves. He agreed to do that. And when I went back to see him a few days later, he immediately told me he has been praying every day all day long for all of us in our chapel community throughout his very painful last days on earth.

Now that Javier has died, we have a friend in heaven. And his work is not going to stop now. He was a good friend to us while he was alive here on earth and will continue to be our friend in heaven. As our friend, he knows all about each one of us and cares about all of our problems. He knows how frustrating life can be in this place. He is well aware of everything you go through every day.

Like the Blessed Mother, who pointed out to Jesus in our Gospel, "They have no more wine," that's what Javier is going to be doing in heaven. It's nice to have friends in high places! That's what the phrase in the Apostles' Creed is all about when it says, "We believe in the communion of saints." We're all one big family—not only here on earth but also in heaven. Death cannot separate us. It cannot make us forget about one another. The love of a family—even this family of faith in Sing Sing—goes beyond the grave and lasts forever.

It hurts to say goodbye to a good friend, but it's important to realize that we haven't lost him. He has simply been released from prison, not only the prison system of New York State, but the prison of his body that had been destroyed by cancer. Now that he is free he can be an even better friend to us than ever before. And we can trust that he will never forget about us.

There were many tears in that chapel that evening, and I choked up on several occasions while struggling to deliver that heartfelt tribute to someone I had gotten to know, not as a convict, but as a friend. I know that if Javier had been able to speak English, and if he had had the money for a good attorney, he would never have been in prison. He had been convicted of killing a man who had attacked him on the street. He was defending his life. But as an undocumented immigrant with no money, he had no justice. And in a prison where people are treated worse than animals by medical professionals who have lost sight of their calling to care for people, he was killed by their callous disregard for the value of life. Tragically, he was just one of many, and because he was "just a prisoner," nobody cared.

After Javier's death I prepared a scrapbook with pictures of him restoring the stained-glass windows and gave it to his brother at the funeral parlor, along with notes of condolences from his friends at Sing Sing, to take with him when he escorted Javier's body back to their parents in Mexico. Stu then took over the stained-glass restoration project, and after completing our windows, he trained the workers from the Protestant chapel and helped them to restore theirs.

8

Transformation

Some of our parishioners had attended Catholic school, and many of them had been baptized and confirmed, but very few of them understood much about their faith. That was why providing some form of religious instruction was a top priority. I experimented with different ways of providing a foundation in basic spirituality. The Wednesday evening mass and Bible study with small-group discussion was one way to give meaning to their faith. Another was film. I had purchased a large collection of movies, documentaries, and dramatized Bible stories, such as *The Ten Commandments,* so I showed religious movies on Thursday evenings. While the movies were playing, I provided counseling and/or confession to individuals who requested them. Toward the end of the evening we discussed the film and what it meant to each of them.

One of their most pressing needs involved dealing with their past. Many suffered from tremendous guilt over what they had done. Some had recurring nightmares and would wake up in the middle of the night screaming as they relived the gory details of their crime over and over. Whenever they would tell me about their nightmares, I would try to help them listen to what God was telling them so they could learn from their mistakes. They needed to make peace with their past so they wouldn't make the same mistakes in the future. They also needed help in rebuilding their lives. Many were alienated from family and friends. Some no longer had families; their parents had died, wives had left them, children and siblings wanted nothing to do with them. Some had nobody on this whole planet who cared whether they lived or died. I vividly remember calling the mother of one of the men to let her know her son had just arrived at Sing Sing, which was very close to where she was living. Her response was, "I never want to hear anything from the prison about my son unless it is to inform me of his death!"

Any religious education program should be designed to make people aware of the love of God, but it was a huge challenge to teach people about God's love when many had experienced so little of it from their own family, which was supposed to be the primary reflection of that love. I tried to create a new family for them within the chapel community where they could escape the hassle of prison life and find peace. It was a place where everybody, regardless of past history, was made to feel welcome and was treated like a child of God. As they got involved in our various chapel activities, and as they interacted with the civilian volunteers who came faithfully to lead small-group discussions, they couldn't help but feel the love of God in our midst. My motto for the chapel was that it was to be "a refuge in the midst of hell." It was the only place in the whole facility where my parishioners felt they were no longer in prison, where they were treated like men instead of prisoners.

CHAPEL ACTIVITIES

Over the years our chapel activities developed and expanded. Maryknoll priests who had worked in the missions in Latin America conducted a Bible discussion group in Spanish. This had a powerful impact on the Hispanics and helped them bond together as a closely knit family within the chapel community.

Other volunteers conducted centering prayer sessions, somewhat like yoga meditation, teaching the men how to rid their minds of the numerous distractions around them in order to center on the Lord. Many of the men found this particular technique very useful during "count time," when they were locked in their cells for half an hour or more three times a day while the whole facility was being counted.

I conducted a training class where our lectors practiced both the English and Spanish readings for Sunday. Most of the men had never done any kind of public speaking and were extremely nervous about getting up in front of their peers to read at mass. We worked to overcome their fears while teaching them how to enunciate clearly and read with expression. It was amazing to see their progress and their growth in self-confidence. They lost their gruff exterior and developed poise, which would be very helpful in job interviews after their release.

Every Saturday morning we had choir rehearsal. Saturday afternoon was for the catechumenate. This was our primary religious education class. Unlike the old-fashioned catechism classes that required memorizing facts about our faith, the focus of our catechumenate was developing a relationship with God. The class was open to anyone who wanted to learn more about his faith, but its primary purpose was to prepare people to receive the sacraments of initiation: baptism, confirmation, and Eucharist. Our catechumenate contained several different courses of study in the fields of scripture and theology.

BIBLE STUDY

Most prisoners, if they had any knowledge of the Bible, approached the Bible literally. They particularly loved the book of Revelation and were eager to talk about the end of the world. As Tony explained, "When you are sentenced to twenty-five years to life in prison, the thought of the end of the world coming soon is very enticing. Everybody is looking for a way to get his sentence shortened."

Unfortunately, with such an approach people often lose sight of the overall significance of the scriptures to their lives today. By marveling over the spectacular miracles that occurred "way back then," they miss out on what God has to say to us about the problems we are encountering today.

I used the Hebrew scriptures (Old Testament) as the basic foundation for our religious studies. But our three-month course, repeated every year, was about relating to those stories from a prisoner's perspective. "The people of Israel," I explained, "were in much the same situation as you men here. They had ignored the warnings of the prophets, just as many of you ignored the warnings of parents, teachers, and friends, and they messed up badly. They ended up in captivity in Babylon. Their homeland was destroyed. They were traumatized and homesick."

Jerry, who had grown up with no religious background of any kind, was preparing for baptism. He was from the Intermediary Care Program and had the mental capacity of a young child. One day he blurted out, "My grandmother always told me not to hang out with those kids in the neighborhood, because they would get me in trouble, and they did. I should have listened to her."

"That's right, Jerry. But now that you are in prison, God hasn't abandoned you, just as God didn't abandon the people of Israel. Instead, God put prophets in their midst in Babylon to help them regain their faith in God and to realize that God still loved them."

"That's what you are doing for us here in prison," Jerry said. "You are a prophet sent by God to show us a better way to live."

"Yes, those prophets back then were just like prison chaplains. The Hebrew scriptures were written to help people back then as well as people today to connect with the stories of their ancestors and recognize where they had gone wrong and how to get back in touch with God."

We ended the course with the story of Adam and Eve, who had listened to the voice of the tempter in the Garden of Eden instead of the word of the Lord. I explained that it isn't just around an apple tree that we hear "Try it, you'll like it" from a tempter.

"That's what my older brother told me when he gave me my first reefer. I was five years old, and it has all been downhill ever since."

"It is because Adam and Eve listened to the word of the tempter instead of the word of the Lord that they were banished from the Garden of Eden, just as the people of Israel were banished from the promised land," I said.

"And that is why we have been banished from our homes to prison," lamented Jerry.

THEOLOGY CLASSES

We had a constant turnover of people coming into the facility and being transferred out. They would join us wherever we happened to be in our classes. Since most of them were with us for close to a year, they eventually got the whole curriculum. In addition to the Bible study, we had three different courses in theology. One was Christology and was intended to help them get to know Jesus Christ, not just as an abstract doctrine, but within the context of a personal relationship. I wanted them to see him not as a dead specimen in a theology book but as a living, personal companion on their journey through life. We also focused on the necessity of cooperating with the word of the Lord so that Jesus Christ could become flesh in our lives, just as he had in Mary's life.

There was also a course in moral theology to learn how to discern right from wrong. "If you were to drop a frog in a pot of boiling water, its reflexes would immediately cause it to jump right out. But if you were to put it in a pot of cold water and very gradually heat it up, it probably wouldn't notice the heat until it was too late. By then its muscles would be so relaxed it could no longer jump," I theorized. Then I hastily assured them that I had never actually *tried* such an experiment and certainly wouldn't recommend that anyone ever torture a creature like that.

"But I get your point," said David, another candidate for baptism. "Most of us would never have chosen early in life to do the things we eventually did that got us locked up. Little by little we made decisions that eventually deadened our consciences and caused us to commit some terrible crimes."

"Exactly. That is why we all need to learn how to discern every step of the way what God wants us to do to prevent anything like that from happening again in the future."

Our course on sacramental theology helped them understand the meaning of the sacraments. "Most people," I pointed out, "tend to think of the sacraments as some form of magic. You take a little baby, add some water, say a few prayers, and you end up with a brand-new Christian.

"Isn't that how it works?" asked Ricky, who was also preparing for baptism.

"No, Ricky. If that were the case, Adolf Hitler, who was a baptized Catholic, would be a saint." Everybody readily agreed that he wasn't, so we didn't have any neo-Nazis in our midst. "There was nothing wrong with the water that was used when Hitler was baptized, but there is far more to being a Christian than getting wet. The same is true for all of the other sacraments. Many people have beautiful wedding celebrations but never learn how to turn their marriage into a sacrament through unconditional love."

"That was the problem with my marriage," Fred said. "My wife never learned how to love. All she knew how to do was make my life miserable."

Everybody groaned. "Here we go, again," sighed David.

"OK, Fred, let's not go there," I said. "We've all heard that story too many times. But it is true that it takes two people working together, cooperating with God to make a marriage work. Similarly, many people go to confession as a means of whitewashing their sins with no intention of changing their behavior, because they don't understand the meaning of conversion. Many people receive communion even though they hate their neighbor."

"So what you are saying, then, is that sacraments require our cooperation," David said. "They don't just happen automatically."

"That's right, David. God stretches out a hand to give us grace through these sacramental moments, but we have to reach out and take that outstretched hand and cooperate with that grace for the sacrament to have any effect on our lives."

During one of our classes someone I had never seen before and who wasn't on the official callout list of people approved to come to the chapel managed to slip past the chapel OIC and join our class. After a few minutes he began to dominate the conversation and grew increasingly more agitated. "I am a prophet sent by God to call you people to repent," he said.

I tried to gently remind him that that was my job, in a futile attempt to regain control of the class, but then he began yelling, stood up and walked toward me, shaking his fist menacingly. Immediately, without any prompting from anyone, the entire class stood up and formed a protective circle around me.

Afterward, Fred explained. "That guy stopped taking his psych meds a few weeks ago, and now he is falling apart."

I thanked Fred for the information and reported the situation to the man's therapist in the hope that the therapist would intervene before anyone got hurt. But it was wonderful to feel the love and protection that those men demonstrated by being willing to place themselves in harm's way to keep that mentally ill man from hurting me.

LEARNING FROM THE LITURGY

The liturgy itself provides many opportunities for religious education and transformation, but only when people understand it. This was why I took great care to explain all of the rituals that we celebrated.

Periodically, we had an "instructional mass," in which a narrator explained what was taking place as the mass was being celebrated. Tony confided in me after the first of these, "I was an altar boy as a kid and knew the whole mass in Latin. I knew exactly what I was supposed to do, but until now I never had any idea what it all meant."

To encourage people to go to confession, we staged a non-sacramental penance service during one of my homilies to teach the men the meaning and purpose of this sacrament. Many of the men had not been to confession since they were children. Not only were they ashamed to confess their sins, but they were embarrassed to admit that they didn't remember how to make a confession. Seeing a staged confession put them at ease and prompted many of them to make use of the sacrament to make peace with God.

One of the most important opportunities for religious education occurs every year with the Rite of Christian Initiation of Adults (RCIA) during the season of Lent. With today's emphasis on infant baptism and communion and confirmation for grade-school children, we tend to lose sight of what it means to be initiated into a community of believers.

Within a prison environment, initiation is about gangs.

Many of our members had been members of various gangs. Although any form of gang activity is prohibited in prison, just as drugs, alcohol, and sexual activity are prohibited, gang membership is an integral part of the prison culture. We had numerous gang members who attended chapel, but not usually for the purpose of praying. This was an easily accessible place to meet one another, hold quick meetings before or after mass, and relay messages and plans.

A few gang members, however, converted from that way of life and became dynamic leaders within the chapel community. One of those former gang members, Packo, due to his age and lengthy time in service, was granted *anciano* status by the gang, meaning he was a revered elder but no longer in active service. As a gang member he had had a long career of sordid crimes and had several tear drops tattooed on his face to indicate the number of people he had killed in the line of duty. But those days were behind him, and he wanted to get right with God. Although all gang activities and ceremonies are kept secret, he shared some of the initiation rite with me, explaining, "You see, Father, if someone wants to join a gang here, he can't simply walk up to the gang leader and ask for an application form."

"Why not?" I asked.

"That would be a good way to get the living shit knocked out of you. That's not how we do things. When I joined, one of the brothers had to sponsor me. My sponsor put his reputation on the line by recommending me as a new member. He had to make sure that I was OK with what our gang stands for. Once he recommended me, I entered a trial period to learn about the brotherhood so the members could check me out. I had to memorize our whole history—where, when, and why we got started—and then be totally committed to that purpose. I had to pledge my absolute obedience to the gang, even being willing to lay down my life for my brothers. During this trial period the other brothers were constantly checking me out to make sure I was an OK dude. But I also had to be sure that this was the kind of life I wanted to live. After several months of this the other dudes decided to put me through the initiation. The ceremony is different for each gang, but it is really powerful and bonds us to one another for life. During the initiation I was tattooed with an emblem of the gang to show that from then on, I belonged to them."

Although tattooing is forbidden, it is widely practiced. Tattoo guns were ingeniously devised from the insert of a ballpoint pen and a sewing needle powered by the motor from a Walkman tape player or hair clippers. The ink was made from burnt dominoes or chess pieces. It is amazing that all of this could occur right in front of the not-too-observant guards in the recreational yard.

I always explained to our prospective converts that the RCIA is actually quite similar to the rite of initiation for most gangs, but I quickly clarified that we have a different gang leader. "For us," I emphasized, "it is all about making a conscious decision to commit ourselves to following the Lord Jesus Christ.

"Do we need to have a sponsor to recommend us?" asked Packo.

"Yes," I told him. "One of the brothers here in our congregation has to sponsor you and help you through our initiation process. You will need to study the history of our 'gang,' the church, find out what our purpose is, and be willing to work together with us to achieve it. And throughout the centuries, many of our members have willingly laid down their lives for the sake of the gospel. It would be absurd to join the Latin Kings or any of the other gangs here in prison without any understanding of what their purpose is. Yet some people have joined the church without even bothering to find out what it means to be a Christian or taking the time to read our 'handbook,' which is the Bible. When you are initiated into Christianity, you will be expected to love your enemies and forgive those who have hurt you. You will also be expected to care about the needs of others, instead of just looking out for your own best interests. If you are not willing to do so, you might want to reconsider applying for membership." We had some people who dropped out, because they were honest enough to recognize that they couldn't make that kind of commitment.

We had a very lengthy course of study to prepare for initiation, but not nearly as lengthy as that required in the early church, when the process lasted at least three years. I wasn't interested in large numbers of converts. I wanted to see them make some drastic changes in their way of life. It was difficult to follow through on those preparing for initiation, because many of them were at Sing Sing for only a year or less. Sometimes we would start out with seven or eight catechumens and candidates in August, but by the time Holy Week arrived the following March or April, almost all of them would have been transferred elsewhere. Sing Sing was their first stop after being processed into the prison system at Downstate Correctional Facility at Fishkill, so many of them only stayed with us for a year before they were sent upstate to other facilities. But I got them started in the right direction and then referred them on to the next chaplain to continue the process. Unfortunately, as I heard from so many of them after their transfer, little if any religious education was offered in many of the other prisons, with the result that some got lost in the shuffle.

For the candidates who remained, the season of Lent was an exciting time in their final preparation for receiving the sacraments of initiation. On the first Sunday of Lent, we celebrated the rite of welcoming, in which we presented them to the congregation along with their sponsors, whom they had selected from among fellow prisoners who were practicing their faith, and they were blessed with the sign of the cross. The following Sunday was the rite of election, when the candidates signed our Book of the Elect on the altar, expressing their commitment to follow the Lord. The last three Sundays of Lent were devoted to scrutinies and exorcisms. These became a very important part of the Lenten journey for the whole chapel as a form of examination of conscience and prayer for deliverance that was beneficial for everyone, not just those preparing to receive the sacraments.

Every year I explained what is meant by *exorcism,* first of all by reassuring them that it is not what they have seen in the movies. I explained that every time a little baby is baptized, there is a prayer of exorcism to set it free from original sin. I also told them that shortly before Mother Teresa died she called for a priest to perform an exorcism over her.

"Well, if Mother Teresa thought she needed an exorcism," Mark said, "an exorcist could have a field day around here. Every time we relapse, it seems like a demon is in control. Will an exorcism help?"

"There are demonic forces all around us continually trying to trip us up," I explained. "We use these exorcisms to set us free from whatever those powerful urges are that cause us to sin. We base those exorcisms each year on three stories from the Gospel of John: The Woman at the Well (John 4), to help us identify unhealthy thirsts that prevent us from finding Living Water; The Man Born Blind (John 9), to help us identify our blind spots; and on the last Sunday of Lent, The Raising of Lazarus (John 11), to help us identify the areas of our lives that are still bound up in grave clothes, preventing us from being free."

At each of those Sunday liturgies, as our converts knelt in front of the altar for the scrutinies and exorcisms, I asked the congregation, usually numbering between sixty and eighty, to extend their hands, not only to pray for the converts, but to open themselves up to the same liberating power of God to set them free from whatever demonic forces were still troubling them.

THE ROSARY

An important aspect of religious education must always include teaching people how to pray. This was especially so in prison, where many of the prisoners had no idea what prayer was or how to begin to get in touch with God. Most of them were familiar with the

Rosary as something to wear around their neck for good luck, but they had no idea how to use it or how to relate the various "mysteries" of the Rosary to their personal experiences, so I designed a Rosary Holy Hour to help them become acquainted with the richness of this tradition. I explained that a Holy Hour is simply spending time with the Lord, who is present in a special way in the Eucharist that is exposed on the altar. There are many ways of doing this. We combined music, scripture readings, prayers of petitions for others, and silent meditation with praying the Rosary.

WHISTLE BLOWING

Shortly after I started working at Sing Sing, I became a whistle-blower in my former parish after discovering that the pastor had molested some of the altar boys. This was a messy situation that was highly publicized in the newspapers and on television. Some of the parishioners on the outside ostracized me, blaming me for stirring up trouble, even though the pastor had been molesting boys in numerous parishes for the past thirty years. People would rather believe that I was lying than that their beloved pastor could do such a thing. Such is the power of denial.

The response inside of the prison, however, was overwhelmingly supportive from prisoners and officers alike. My good friend Sergeant Coop told me that if I ever experienced any reprisals from the archdiocese for taking such a public stand, she would arrange to have a whole delegation of officers go down to the cathedral to picket on my behalf. I told her that wouldn't be necessary, but I thanked her profusely for her offer and was genuinely moved by it. One of the prisoners whom I had never even met came up to me in the corridor and told me he just wanted to shake my hand for what I had done. He said that if a priest had stood up for him like that when he was a kid he never would have ended up in prison.

The publicity that came from my whistleblowing status brought a lot of prisoners to my office with a story to share about how they had been abused as children, in some cases by priests. Most of them had never shared that experience with anyone else, but had kept it as a deeply buried secret throughout their lives. That secret had been like a cancer in their soul, slowly destroying them from the inside out. Most of them had quickly turned to alcohol and other drugs as a means of blotting out the pain, eventually leading them to prison. Talking about that experience, often for the first time in their lives, helped them understand why they had done the things that they had done. Convinced that there were plenty of others who had not yet talked about their past abuse, I used our religious education program to address the problem head on by showing the 1997 movie *Good Will Hunting*. Like the psychiatrist, who reassured the troubled young Will Hunting that the physical abuse he had suffered from his father wasn't his fault, I tried to convince these troubled victims of sexual abuse, and other abuse as well, that it wasn't their fault either. Many of them had lived with guilt all their lives for something that had been done to them, often by a close relative. Since they were not capable of dealing with that experience at a young age, most simply locked it up in the deep recesses of their mind and tried to forget all about it. Once they were able to look at it objectively as an adult, they were able to begin their journey toward liberation and healing. Since we had a constant changeover of parishioners, I showed *Good Will Hunting* in the chapel at least once a year. I always asked the men afterward if they could guess why I would show such a profanity-laced movie in our chapel, and almost always they would guess it was because of that powerful scene when Robin Williams as the psychiatrist repeats over and over, "It wasn't your fault." That truly touched the depths of their being.

9

Retreats

A retreat is a group withdrawal for prayer, meditation, or study, usually to a place that offers seclusion. We were allowed to have two chapel retreats every year. Obviously, we could not take the men to an outside retreat house, so we held the retreats in the chapel itself. We pushed the pews to the back of the chapel and had the men sit around tables in the front. The retreat in the fall was for three days, during which time the men were in the chapel from 8:30 a.m. until 8:30 p.m., while the one in the spring was for just one day. As long as they were in the chapel, they were away from all of the harassment of their daily routine. I chose a theme for each retreat based on what the community needed at the moment. Some of our retreat themes were "Addiction and Liberation," "Forgiveness," "Building a Community," "Shalom," and "Prayer."

In the beginning the retreats were conducted by outside team members, and then by our chapel volunteers. But toward the end almost all of our retreats were done by members of our chapel. Working together as a team and developing their talks around specific themes was not only therapeutic for the team members, but most important, their personal witness talks had a profound impact on the retreatants.

One of the problems we confronted was the sense of division between the Latinos and the non-Latinos. I had been encouraged by other chaplains when I first arrived to have two separate masses— one in English and one in Spanish. I adamantly refused, insisting that we were one community that happened to speak two different languages. All of our masses and retreats were conducted bilingually for that reason. However, it wasn't easy to get people from different ethnic and cultural backgrounds to interact. They didn't mix in the rest of the prison (or in the outside world), and it was difficult to get them to do so in the chapel. One particular retreat theme was designed to motivate them to try to connect with one another.

BUILDING A COMMUNITY

When the men gathered on the first day of the retreat, they sat in groups with their friends. As usual, the Hispanics sat together, so they could conduct their discussions in Spanish. As an icebreaker, we had each person in the group introduce himself at the table and tell one thing of interest about himself that no one else knew. Then they were to come up with a name for the group that would reflect something unique about it, after which each group introduced all of its members and explained why the members had selected that name.

I gave the opening talk, focusing on the positive, showing the progress they had already made in building up the community. This was followed by witness talks by several of our members who shared how being a part of the Catholic community had helped to change their lives. Each talk was followed by small-group discussions that were later summarized for the large group in English and Spanish.

The second day was about obstacles to community. We focused on various problem areas that interfered with our ability to interact with one another. Different members highlighted various obstacles. The first obstacle was the language barrier, and the talk was given by José, one of our bilingual Puerto Rican members who had completed the NYTS master's program.

José said: "We need to stop thinking in terms of 'them and us' but rather to see one another as members of one big family regardless of our ethnic background or language. As part of this family, we should all want to get to know one another. We may never be capable of an in-depth technical conversation, but we can at least communicate our love, appreciation, and respect for one another. Lots of our brethren are bilingual and capable of translating, so make use of us in relating with those who don't speak your language." He also encouraged the non-Spanish speakers to try to learn a few Spanish words and for the Spanish men, almost all of whom understood a little English, not to be afraid to use their broken "Spanglish" to communicate.

The second obstacle was mental illness. Because the Office of Mental Health runs a Psychiatric Satellite Unit (PSU) at Sing Sing to provide psychological treatment, we had a high percentage of prisoners with various mental problems in our population, and many of them attended our chapel. One of our men, Nick, after completing the NYTS master's program, was assigned a job working in the ICP, so he described the difficulties many of the men with mental illness had in fitting in with the rest of the community. Some of them were participating in the retreat. Nick helped people understand some of the problems of mental illness and some of the horrible experiences many had endured in their childhood: "Many of these men have been ridiculed all of their lives because of their illness. It's not their fault that they are bipolar or schizophrenic or that many were never diagnosed or treated for their illnesses. Coming to the chapel is a refuge for them, and the last thing they need to find here is more ridicule or rejection for being different. They are our brothers, and we need to look out for them and make them feel welcome and safe within our family."

The third obstacle to community involved people's attitude toward sex offenders. This was a huge problem. In the prison system sex offenders are at the very bottom of the pecking order. Murderers, gangsters, and bank robbers subscribe to a prison code that dictates that no one should talk to or have anything to do with anyone convicted of a sex crime. When sex offenders are out in the recreational yard, they are not allowed to associate with anyone at the tables. They are like lepers, shunned by all. I had caused quite an uproar shortly after my arrival by defending everyone's right to attend chapel services. Indeed, many of the older prisoners with life sentences left in disgust and some never returned.

At the retreat one of the returning old-timers related: "I used to take it upon myself to run sex offenders out of the chapel, threatening to beat the shit out of them if they ever came back. But when I started reading the Bible, I saw that my crime of murder is no better than theirs. Even though the prison code demands that we have nothing to do with them, that code was designed by criminals. Here in this chapel we follow God's code, revealed to us by Jesus, who demands that his followers love one another and refrain from judging one another."

I then told a story about a young man who had been convicted of raping and murdering his high-school classmate. When he came to Sing Sing (before my arrival) he was shunned by all of the "holier than thou" members of the Catholic chapel and ended up joining the Muslims, who accepted him. Many years later he was exonerated of the crime and set free. I reminded them that the Innocence Project has helped to exonerate many unjustly convicted prisoners through

DNA and that nobody really knows who is guilty and who might actually be innocent. I also expressed hope that in the future, when someone is exonerated for a crime he didn't commit, he would leave prison thankful for the love and support he had received in our chapel community.

At the end of the day we had another icebreaker. By this time the men had absorbed enough of the retreat material to make a huge difference in their interactions with one another. Instead of allowing them to continue sitting with their friends and with those who spoke the same language, we did our own version of the childhood game "fruit basket upset" in order to mix up the seating arrangement and force them to mingle with others. It was amazing to see how easily they were then able to relate to people who previously had been outside their comfort zone.

The third day focused on how we could implement what we had learned in our chapel community. We discussed our vision of the community as a refuge in the midst of hell and sought suggestions about how we could better fulfill that vision. We listed the benefits of belonging to this community as well as the obligations we needed to accept in order to continue the building process. We had some lively discussions, and José remarked: "It seems like a spirit of brotherly love has come upon us in a way that I have never experienced before during the past twenty years that I have been in prison."

Instead of a group of Hispanics talking among themselves in one corner, white murderers talking in another, people with mental problems in another, and sex offenders in another, those lines started blurring, and the men began intermingling as one big family.

DAYS OF RECOLLECTION

Every spring we had a day of recollection, basically a one-day retreat. Some were miniature versions of the retreat described above, with talks by various members of the chapel followed by discussions in small groups. At other times I invited outside speakers to offer presentations on a topic of interest.

Ray Boswell, a potter, came in on a couple of occasions to demonstrate with his potter's wheel how God forms our lives. His presentations were among the most popular. It was fascinating to watch him put a blob of clay on the wheel and mold it into all kinds of beautiful vessels, explaining how God forms each one of us throughout our lives. Then he asked if any of the men would like to try their hand at it. What had looked so easy was far from it. Time after time, all they could do was make a mess! Then Ray explained that first the clay must be centered on the wheel, just as our lives must be centered on God. That alone, however, was not enough to turn them into expert potters. Then he placed his hands on theirs, and much to their delight, together they were able to create something beautiful.

I readily identified with the potter's role in the chapel. Most of the parishioners were badly misshapen blobs of clay. Few of them had ever been "centered" on anything other than drugs, alcohol, greed, or bottled-up anger. Most of their past formation had been done by very inexperienced "hands." My role was to allow the hands of God to work through my hands to reform these men in the love of God. The primary goal of everything I did in the prison was to introduce (or reintroduce) those misshapen blobs of clay to the one true God, whom most of them had previously known only as a swear word.

For another day of recollection I invited a woman to come in and speak about the importance of prayer in her life. That might sound like a rather dull topic for a group of prisoners, but her witness story was anything but dull. After only ten years of marriage, and with three young children, her husband had a stroke that left him with the mental capacity of a five-year-old. He eventually regained his physical health, but he needed constant care and supervision. She became the sole breadwinner for the family, working two jobs to make ends meet. In addition, she cared for the children and did all of the household chores, including learning how to fix the toilet since she couldn't afford to hire a plumber. Her husband got his days and nights mixed up and would sleep all day while the caregiver was there but be up all night when she needed to sleep.

This went on for twenty-three years, until he died. Through it all, the only thing that kept her sane was prayer. She told the men that her children could tell by her attitude whether or not she had prayed that day and often would interrupt her to say, "Mom, you need to pray."

The men were overwhelmed by her presentation and gave her a standing ovation, since very few of them had ever experienced such unconditional love from anyone in their entire lives. Having been so deprived of love, they needed to hear someone else's experience of what true love is, as well as to hear how prayer could help them cope with the hardships in their lives.

10

Addiction and Liberation

Addiction is a major problem in our whole society, but it is especially prevalent in prison. There was an inexhaustible supply of drugs in Sing Sing, smuggled into the facility in a variety of ways and sold surreptitiously in the recreational yards, school, housing blocks, and even in the hospital and chapel. Numerous times I felt I was reenacting the gospel story of Jesus driving the moneychangers out of the Temple when I confronted drug dealers in the chapel. For several weeks in a row some of the drug dealers decided to transact business in the back row of the chapel during Sunday mass. This was one of the few times that I tried to get the administration to help me address a problem, which was a sign of how desperate I was. I explained what was going on and asked that they provide an officer to sit in the back of the chapel during mass. The response was that they didn't have enough officers for that, but that they would see that the men were searched after they left the chapel. This plan was not the way to catch the dealers—only the customers.

I realized that I would have to take care of the problem myself, so I went out of my way to make the drug dealers feel unwelcome. Instead of beginning mass at the altar, as usual, I stood in the back of the chapel, right next to the dealers, and glared straight at them throughout the first part of the mass. When I said, "The Lord be with you," I bent over and had my face right up to theirs. My homily began with the following announcement:

"For any of you who came here today for the purpose of copping drugs from our local drug dealers, let me assure you that those people are not your friends. They are simply making a lot of money off of your problem. But if you continue to do business with them, sooner or later you will end up in the Box, and you will continue to disappoint your family members who love you. Stay away from these bastards! Let them keep their drugs so that they are the ones who will get caught with them. Don't take the evidence off their hands."

And during the Prayer of the Faithful one of my petitions was this:

"For all who are engaged in selling drugs within this chapel, that they be caught and sent to the Box and then shipped as far away from here as possible, let us pray to the Lord."

My war with the drug dealers was the talk of Sing Sing. The regular parishioners were afraid to confront them, because this would get them killed, but privately they cheered me on. Word got back to me that the drug dealers were upset that I had called them bastards from the altar.

"I was only calling them what they are," was my response.

After a few weeks the dealers got tired of my persecuting them and left us alone, much to everyone's relief. Fortunately, there were no fights, no stabbings, and no one got into any kind of trouble. Unfortunately, the dealers simply found a more hospitable location to do business. Their next stop was the Quakers, who had no chaplain to harass them.

ADDICTION IS A DISEASE

Since time immemorial society, failing to understand that addiction is a disease, has considered any form of addiction to be a moral failing. We cannot "cure" that disease by locking up people in prison or by shunning them as outcasts. People need treatment in a healthy, therapeutic environment. Unfortunately, our society chooses to put them in a corrupt prison system that hires incompetent, untrained workers who only make the problem worse instead of treating the cause of the problem.

Although well over half of the people in prison have substance abuse or addiction problems, in New York State the usual protocol requires them to wait until they are within two years of being released from prison before they can participate in the mandated drug treatment program. So, if a person is sentenced to twenty-five years to life for murdering someone while high on drugs, he may have to wait twenty-three years to get help with his drug problem. Even then, however, like so many mandated state programs, the quality of the program is usually dubious. In many prisons it is common knowledge that the best place to find a drug supplier is in the drug treatment program. For untreated addicts who know nothing about the principles of recovery, being in the presence of drugs on a daily basis means that many will give in to temptation.

At one of our State Catholic Chaplains' annual retreats I asked Commissioner Fischer why the mandated drug program started so late in the sentence. He replied that when they had offered the program earlier in the sentence, too many of the program's graduates ended up relapsing and having to take the program over and over again. So, they decided to make them wait until later so they would have to take it only once. Sadly, drug treatment programs overall have not been very successful in helping addicts overcome their addictions.

In the 1990s New Jersey had a strict zero-tolerance policy for drugs in prison. Any prisoner who was caught with drugs had all visits suspended for a year. If there was a repeat violation, visits were suspended for the duration of the sentence. There was a similar policy for staff members. Everybody had a powerful incentive to behave. In New York, prisoners caught with what was commonly referred to as a "dirty urine" in a random drug test are sent to the Box. A first offense usually costs them three months in the Box and loss of packages and phone privileges for an additional three months. The penalty increases with future offenses. However, they rarely lose highly coveted visiting privileges, even when they are in the Box, although they are limited to only one visit per week. Both of these methods, however, are strictly punitive, not rehabilitative.

Sing Sing is the maximum-security prison closest to New York City, where the vast majority of the prisoners are from. Such a desirable location would make it an ideal choice for an honor facility. Only those prisoners who have maintained a clean disciplinary record and have completed their required programs should be allowed to be transferred there, where they can have family visits every day of the week. That would be a tremendous incentive to behave. Instead, almost half of the prison population consists of people who have just begun their sentence and stay at Sing Sing only for six to twelve months before being transferred upstate. Many of them are young punks who are members of gangs and have serious drug problems. They should be sent upstate for their preliminary programs, including drug treatment. Only after the successful completion of those programs and only with a clean disciplinary record should they become eligible for an honor facility. Currently, the presence of so many out-of-control addicts makes the place a living hell for everyone. What exacerbates the problem even more is that Sing Sing is used as a training facility for new officers fresh from the training academy. Most of the new officers stay for about a year and then are transferred elsewhere. The result is a constant changeover of inexperienced staff in charge of a constantly changing population of undisciplined drug addicts. The result is chaos.

Unfortunately, since most of the officers are from upstate, Sing Sing is not a popular assignment. As soon as they get enough seniority, they transfer closer to home. That is why so many new officers are sent there. But responsible supervisors, properly compensated, could make a huge difference in teaching those new officers how to run an honor facility.

DRUGS IN PRISON

Prison counselors, like all other state workers, are a mixture of good, bad, and indifferent. Few of them have any training in addiction counseling or any other kind of counseling. They are only required to see the prisoners on their caseloads three or four times a year for approximately ten minutes each time to see if they want any additions to their approved phone list, which is a prerequisite for making collect phone calls. During that brief session they also check to see what mandated programs they still need to enroll in before their release. In all fairness, it must be acknowledged that some of them go far beyond the call of duty in trying to help their clients and are truly unsung heroes within the system. But most are not heroic. The same is true of the trained social workers in mental health. Many therapists are eager to prescribe medications, but very few are willing to take the time to listen.

With hundreds of untreated addicts in the prison and a readily available supply of illegal drugs to satisfy their urges, this can hardly be considered a therapeutic or correctional environment. When most of the inmates are eventually released from prison, they still haven't learned to cope with those insatiable urges. It is not surprising that the recidivism rate is deplorable.

Great precautions are understandably taken to search visitors coming into the facility to make sure they are not smuggling in drugs. Even so, people keep trying, and sometimes they manage to hide drugs, perhaps in condoms that they insert in bodily cavities or even in a baby's diaper. If they are successful in getting the drugs in, the prisoners take the drugs into the bathroom and insert them up their rectum or even swallow the condom and allow nature to take its course the following day.

However, the visitors are frequently arrested when their attempts are discovered. I vividly recall an elderly Hispanic woman sobbing hysterically after being caught trying to smuggle in drugs for her son. Her infant grandson was still with her as she waited for the State Police to arrive and arrest her and take her to the county jail. The poor woman's life was ruined. I was disgusted with her son for putting his mother and son in such a position.

Since there were elaborate screening methods in place for detecting drugs, it was impossible for so many to get in without considerable "cooperation" within the system. Some of Sing Sing's officers came from the same neighborhoods in New York City as many of the prisoners, and some were even from the same street gangs, so they brought the drugs in themselves for their "homeboys." Since the officers were never searched when they entered the facility, this was easily done. They provided drugs and alcohol to their homeboys, who then served as dealers for the other prisoners, selling their wares for three to four times the customary price on the street. The dealers usually enlisted the help of others, including gang members, to carry the drugs out to the yard to distribute to their numerous customers. A prisoner could go shopping for his drug of choice out in the yard once he had the right contacts and followed the required protocol.

This was a lucrative business for everyone involved. Methods of payment varied. For marijuana, people paid with the usual currency of cigarettes, preferably Newports. Since heroin was much more expensive, the prisoners had to have someone on the outside send a money order to a PO Box for the dealer's wife or girlfriend. She, in turn, would send a generous amount of money to the dealer, and also make sure that the officer who provided the drugs got his due reward. The system worked well, and many people got wealthy from it, while others became increasingly enslaved by addiction. Since the prisoners made only a few dollars a week, they obviously could not afford drugs without help from the outside. Some had family members who sent them a monthly allowance that financed their drug habit. Others worked as "mules," transporting the drugs from the dealer to the customers in exchange for a share in the merchandise.

But as their habit increases, so does their drug use and their debt. Frequently, addicts will beg their family and friends to bail them out "just one more time" to avoid being slashed in the face by a gang member who is hired to settle such scores. If they are slashed, they end up in protective custody, either involuntarily or voluntarily. If they go voluntarily, it means they "ratted out" the person who slashed them, and they are labeled a snitch for the rest of.their time in prison.

ADDICTION AND LIBERATION RETREAT

After seeing so many of my parishioners get into trouble for a "dirty urine," I developed a retreat called Addiction and Liberation. Unlike our earlier retreats, which usually were organized by an outside team of speakers, this one was the first to feature witness talks given exclusively by the men themselves. The participants were assigned to specific groups with a fellow prisoner who had been trained as a facilitator for each group. After every talk the groups discussed how they reacted to what was shared. After approximately twenty minutes of small-group discussion, each table sent a representative to summarize for the whole community what its group had discussed. Then each group collaborated on drawing a poster to illustrate what the members had learned from the talk. These posters were later explained to the community. Some groups could rival Michelangelo while others used stick figures, but regardless of the quality of the art, many were profound illustrations of the insights they had gained. At the same time, these "art shows" often produced moments of hilarity, team bonding, and friendly rivalry.

At the end of this retreat Tony was in tears as he confided, "This retreat has given me a totally new outlook on my addiction. I have wallowed in shame for years about how I allowed crack cocaine to destroy my life. I thought I became a junkie because I was a bad person."

Many others had the same reaction. Their relapses in prison had been a source of great shame and frustration to them as well as to their families.

Tony summed up the general consensus when he testified at the end of the retreat, "This has helped all of us gain a much better understanding of the nature of our problem and has also given us some tools to help us learn how to cope with it."

11

Forgiveness

Forgiveness is a key element in prisoners' capacity to be rehabilitated. Prisoners need to be forgiven for what they have done, but they also need to learn to forgive others who have hurt them throughout their lives. Most of them have bottled up a lot of anger that spills over into violence and gets them into trouble. Simply locking them up doesn't solve the problem. The rage just continues to simmer and will only get worse unless they find a way to resolve it. Unfortunately, many simply try to repress that anger, especially when they are trying to get back in touch with God, thinking it is unacceptable to be angry at the people who have hurt them.

In counseling numerous men at Sing Sing I frequently discovered they had been abused as children by one or both of their parents. Some were so badly beaten they urinated and defecated in their pants. Others could hardly walk afterward. Johnny, a twenty-eight-year-old man, originally assured me, "I had a reasonably good childhood. It was nothing like what some of these other guys have experienced. There were times when I had some difficulties with my parents, and they were kind of hard on me, but that was because I was always getting into trouble."

After a while, however, I discovered how badly he had been abused by his father, when he confided, "It wasn't just the beatings. What was even worse was when he publicly ridiculed me for wetting the bed. He actually brought the yellow-stained sheets outside when I was waiting for the school bus and waved them at my friends, telling them I still wet the bed. Other times, he would send me to bed without supper or lock me out of the house for infractions of the rules."

But even as he was relating such stories of abuse, Johnny, like so many others, constantly made excuses for his parents: "They were just trying to straighten me out. They didn't do anything that I didn't deserve. I was just a bad kid."

When I kept insisting that this was child abuse and was totally unacceptable, he claimed to have forgiven his parents for their failures. "But forgiveness," I emphasized, "is often a lengthy process, not something we say once, and then it's all over. We have to work on it and struggle with it before we are able to resolve the anger we so rightfully experience after having been hurt and abused."

Johnny had developed an almost Jekyll-and-Hyde personality. Externally he was trying to be a dutiful, loving son and good Christian, but internally he was seething with rage over what had been done to him as a child. He appeared to be a nice, friendly young man, but whenever someone pushed the wrong button he would explode into uncontrollable rage, which was how he (and so many others) had landed in prison and why so many would continue to get into fights with other prisoners.

"You need to listen to that inner child who is still inside of you crying out for justice," I advised him."You need to learn to express what that poor abused child feels about the past, instead of just glossing over it and pretending like everything is now fine." I then asked him, "Have you ever heard of the Stockholm Syndrome?"

Johnny, who was well read with an avid interest in psychology, said, "You mean when captives identify with and bond with their captors and defend them from their liberators?"

"Exactly," I said. "You have been defending your abusers, even though their abuse was inexcusable and against the law. You need to try to break free from their influence."

That was the message that got through to Johnny. For the first time in his life he realized that his parents were wrong and that he had been abused. That was a turning point in his life. While previously he had been frustrated by the lack of support from his parents, such as them not accepting his phone calls or responding to his letters or sending him money for commissary, after this revelation he saw them for what they were and lowered his expectations. After his mother died, he stopped trying to communicate with his father and just wrote him off as a deadbeat dad whom he no longer needed or wanted in his life. He wasn't yet ready to forgive his abusers, but he had taken a major step in the right direction by identifying the abuse.

I brought in a dynamic speaker named Antoinette Bosco to talk about her own struggle with forgiveness. She told how her son and daughter-in-law had been murdered in their home in Montana by a drug-crazed young man. Although she had always been an outspoken opponent of capital punishment, it still was not easy to write to the judge and ask that the person who had killed her loved ones be spared from the death penalty. But she had decided that she didn't want to allow that misguided young man to determine who she was or to control her actions in the future. She knew that the only way she could be free was to forgive him. But she told us that every morning when she woke up, she had to decide whether she wanted to lapse back into anger and be miserable or to forgive and be at peace. "When Jesus told Simon Peter to forgive seventy times seven times," she explained, "who could have imagined that we might have to do that every day? But I just keep on forgiving until the rage stops and I am at peace."

The men were overwhelmed by her presentation and asked her many questions. Most of them had never been forgiven for the crimes they committed, so they found it especially liberating to hear how Antoinette had been able to forgive someone who had caused her so much pain. She gave us one of her books, *Choosing Mercy*, for our library, and she was a topic of conversation for years to come, even among men who had never met her but had read her book.

After hearing her talk, one of the men composed the following letter, edited here for space, which he asked me to send anonymously to the parish of his crime victim. It was totally unsolicited, and he chose to remain anonymous so no one would think he had any ulterior motive for writing.

To the community that I have hurt:

Many years ago, I took the life of a member of your community. Although I was just out of my teens when I committed the crime, this was no excuse. Although I cannot change the events that led to this terrible act, I have learned to take responsibility for my actions. Within this prison environment, filled with killings, stabbings, riots, rapes, and beatings, I have tried to change my life. While serving time in the Box, I came to realize that something was wrong with me. By going through riots and gang wars and by seeing the deaths of others, I came to understand that life is truly precious and that human beings are not meant to hurt one another.

Like so many others, I came from an abusive background filled with physical, emotional, and sexual abuse. This forced me to grow up before my time, forgoing most of my childhood. I learned to hate while most children were learning math and science. I understood that hurt and pain were something you were supposed to endure in silence. My understanding of being a man meant physically abusing the ones I loved or anyone else who got in the way. As a child I lived with the pain of seeing my mother and sister abused by my stepfather and was too small to do anything about it. Due to sexual abuse, I doubted my own masculinity. The fear, pain, and embarrassment I felt caused me to bottle up my problems. I never spoke to anyone about that terrible secret. I was afraid of what others would think if they found out. I did anything I could to prove to myself and to others that I was really a boy.

As I grew older, this mindset never left me. I remained illiterate, with no vocational skills, addicted to drugs, and with a need to prove myself. Out of this background, fueled by greed, anger, and ignorance, I caused the death of one of God's children. I do not know the words to adequately express the remorse I feel. Every day since my awakening, I have asked God and the person I killed for forgiveness.

However, asking for forgiveness by saying "I am sorry" was not the only thing I could do. Since I cannot change the past, I have changed the present by the way I live in prison. I have learned that to be a better person, I must take responsibility for my deeds, both past and present. Then I must do what I can to set things right. I cannot bring back the victim of my crime, but I am doing all I can to help those around me learn from my mistakes. Perhaps some of those reading this letter have suffered the pain of losing a loved one due to the violent act of another. I hope that my apology may help you with the process of healing, and I pray that you may find peace.

This man completed his GED and then went on to get a college degree while in prison. He has since been paroled and is living a productive life.

TIMOTHY MCVEIGH

When Timothy McVeigh went on trial for the Oklahoma City bombing, many prisoners were ready to lynch him themselves because of the heinousness of his crime. This became a teachable moment on the importance of forgiveness. During the month before his execution we began praying for his conversion at every mass. We also prayed for the families of the victims, recognizing the pain that he had inflicted upon them, but I reminded the men that just as people had prayed for their conversion, we needed to pray for Timothy McVeigh to get ready to meet God. After his execution we offered a mass for him at which I gave the following homily:

> One of the witnesses at the execution remarked afterward, "Now Timothy McVeigh is in hell." I can understand people's hurt and bitterness toward him because of his horrible crime, but it is important to remember that we are not the judge who makes the decision about whether a person goes to hell or to heaven. Only almighty God knows what was in Timothy McVeigh's heart. We can only guess. People think he was unrepentant, and he certainly *seemed* that way. He also claimed to be an agnostic and scoffed about going to hell. But the news media reported that at the last minute he called for a priest, the prison chaplain, to give him the last rites. That is not something an agnostic would likely do.
>
> During the past month we in this chapel, along with many others throughout the world, prayed for his conversion. This report would seem to be an answer to our prayers. Part of the last rites involves repentance and forgiveness. Some might say "too little too late." But that is for God to decide, not

us. According to Jesus, in the parable of The Workers in the Vineyard, even those who came at the last minute received the same wages as those who had worked all day.

Some people resent the thought that Timothy McVeigh might get the same heavenly reward as someone who spent his entire life serving God and helping others. But such an attitude implies that living a good life is a waste of time, and that living like the devil is preferable. That is simply not true. I'm quite happy with my way of life. I find great joy and fulfillment in serving God. But when I die, if I bump into Timothy McVeigh in heaven, I won't feel cheated. If anything, *he* is the one who was cheated out of a lifetime of joy and fulfillment because he waited so long to come into the vineyard. It is not up to us to judge what went on inside of Timothy McVeigh's heart. But we must never forget that in spite of all he did, God never for one moment stopped loving him. And it is God's desire that *all* of us—even Timothy—turn to him to be saved. If he took only one tiny step toward God during those last minutes of his life, that is all God needed to reach out and pull him away from the fires of hell.

We all wish Timothy had taken a lot more steps, like apologizing and admitting he was wrong. Obviously, he was not that far along on his journey yet. Receiving those last rites didn't immediately transform him into a full-fledged saint. But it was a start in the right direction. Now, it is up to us to continue to pray for him, as the soldiers in our First Reading 2 Maccabees prayed for their comrades who had died in sin, that even now, after death, Timothy will continue the journey he has just begun, recognizing the horror of his sinful actions and allowing his hatred to be transformed into love, until he is eventually ready to meet God face to face.

Word got back to the Exec Team from one of the prison snitches that we had conducted a funeral service for Timothy McVeigh, and I was called on the carpet. I explained that praying for the dead is an important part of our faith, and that I wanted to teach my congregation the importance of praying for the conversion of criminals, regardless of how notorious their crimes were.

HEALING OF MEMORIES THROUGH FORGIVENESS

An important aspect of forgiveness often requires the healing of painful memories. South African Anglican priest Father Michael Lapsley was involved in the fight against apartheid. As a result, someone sent him a letter bomb in 1990 that blew off both of his hands and blinded him in one eye. After his lengthy recovery he founded the Healing of Memories Institute and teaches people around the world how to forgive so that their painful memories can be healed. I attended one of his workshops at Fordham University in New York and was extremely impressed and eager to bring him into Sing Sing to help our men. Unfortunately, the administration wouldn't allow him in because of the "potential danger" his artificial limbs might pose, but the rest of his team came in and did a one-day workshop with our chapel community. The participants were carefully selected, because the process involved talking about some painful personal details. Some people were not capable of being so open, and others were not trustworthy enough to maintain confidentiality. The retreat began with everyone creating a timeline, drawing the story of his life on a large piece of poster paper. Then each person took a turn explaining what the poster represented. That process lasted several hours. During that time there were lots of tears and hugs, and a quiet peacefulness descended on the chapel as years of hatred and resentment began to melt away. Forgiveness is truly liberating. It wasn't just the prison bars that had been holding them captive. A lifetime of grudges, hatred, and simmering anger had destroyed their freedom long before they arrived in prison. But once they learned to forgive, they found the key that sets captives free.

THE DIVISION OF PAROLE'S RELUCTANCE TO FORGIVE

Perhaps nowhere is a lack of forgiveness more evident than in the Division of Parole. When a person is sentenced, the judge usually gives a minimum and a maximum number of years of incarceration. For example, a person who commits a murder is typically sentenced to twenty-five years to life. That means that in twenty-five years the person is eligible for parole. For many years it was presumed that if a person behaved himself throughout his incarceration, if he took all of the required programs and demonstrated that he was rehabilitated, he would be paroled after completing his minimum sentence of twenty-five years. But if a person was a troublemaker and showed no signs of rehabilitation, he could be kept in prison for the rest of his life—or until he convinced the Parole Board he had truly changed. That flexibility was a powerful incentive for people to behave.

All of that changed with the Pataki administration and its "get tough on crime" policy. From then on, it became politically taboo to release a violent offender because of the "nature of the crime." Murder is obviously a violent crime. Because of its violent nature, the parole commissioners have now replaced the judge and jury in determining what an appropriate sentence should be. For some crimes a judge may sentence the person to life in prison without parole. That is the judge's prerogative. But it is not the prerogative of parole commissioners to resentence a person. Yet I know people who have been "hit" by the board with two more years after each of ten parole appearances, thus adding twenty more years to the judge's original sentence, even though they never had any disciplinary problems and used their prison time productively to help others.

In Jim Murphy's address to the New York State Assembly Standing Committee on Correction on December 4, 2015, he quoted Judge Richard Bartlett, the chair of the Bartlett Commission, which drafted the Criminal Procedure Law of 1971. In a 2010 interview, Bartlett said: "It is not the function of the Board to review the appropriateness of the sentence. That is for the court to decide. Their role is to determine the suitability of release based on the inmate's behavior while imprisoned and the likelihood of their reoffending."

Yet, as reported by John Caber in the September 16, 2013, *New York Law Journal,* Robert Dennison, a former chairman of the Parole Commission, said, "If the Parole Board doesn't like the crime, you are not going to get out."

No one can change the past. The crimes that some people have committed are truly horrible. But if the goal of a correctional facility is to correct a person's behavior, and if that person's behavior truly is corrected, that should be the determining factor for parole. The current obsession of the parole commissioners with keeping people convicted of violent crimes locked up forever is a violation of their original sentence. What is even more disturbing is that many of the people convicted of so-called nonviolent crimes, like drug dealers, are far more likely to reoffend than any of the violent felons. Statistics from New York State Department of Corrections, quoted on their website, Appendix C of "1985–2010 Releases Most Serious Crimes of Commitment by Return Type"—show that of 2,410 prisoners with murder convictions who were released during that time frame, 388 returned to prison. Of those who returned, only 48, a mere 2 percent of all those released, were returned for a new conviction; the others were returned for parole violations (14 percent). Compare this with the 40 percent of drug felons released in 2010 who were returned to prison within three years.

Many of those "nonviolent" drug dealers are in and out of prison, and every time they get out they go right back to their lucrative business of selling the drugs that led the majority of the prisoners to commit the crimes that brought them to prison. As for the "violent" offenders, their offense usually occurred during one moment of passion when for whatever reason their lives got out of control and they committed a terrible act that brought them to prison. The crimes they committed were violent, but the perpetrators are not necessarily violent persons, and when they come to their senses, most are no longer violent. If the goal of a correctional facility is to correct criminal behavior, one would think that the Parole Board would release those whose behavior has been corrected. Yet many offenders sit in prison for ten or twenty years after their minimum sentence, while the drug dealers, whose behavior has remained uncorrected, are right back in business in your neighborhood. I had an opportunity to address some of the members of the Parole Board at Eastern Correctional Facility on behalf of a man who had previously been at Sing Sing. As a youth he had been involved in a robbery that resulted in a death. After he had been "hit" with additions to his sentence at the board numerous times, this time they listened, and the man was finally set free.

A LESSON IN FORGIVENESS FROM RWANDA

A major turning point in my life came when I had the opportunity to learn firsthand about the prison system in Rwanda. My colleague from the Protestant chapel, Father Petero Sabune, an Anglican priest, invited me in 2007 to go with him to Rwanda to work with prisoners who had committed genocide. He had received a grant from Trinity Church in Manhattan for the project and invited me, along with another prison chaplain, to go with him.

On our first trip to Rwanda, in July 2007, we met with government officials from the National Unity and Reconciliation Commission, as well as with religious leaders who were involved in the process of reconciling survivors with the perpetrators of the genocide. We also toured the prison system and met with prison officials as well as with some of the 120,000 *genocidaires* who were imprisoned in their fourteen prisons. We were extremely impressed by all that we witnessed. Their government had quickly realized that without forgiveness and reconciliation, sooner or later another genocide would be inevitable. Such a prospect was unthinkable, so the government made this a major priority and established the National Unity and Reconciliation Commission in its constitution. Because Rwanda is a poor country, it couldn't afford the "luxury" of keeping people locked up forever, so the primary goal was to rehabilitate them. Since most of the *genocidaires* had been brainwashed into thinking it was their patriotic duty to get rid of their Tutsi neighbors, they had to be deprogrammed of those racist tendencies so they could see the error of their ways. Then they were encouraged to ask forgiveness of the families of their victims. Meanwhile, clergy on the outside worked with the victims' families to help them recognize the importance of forgiveness in order to find peace.

There was a wonderful program run by Prison Fellowship, in which a prisoner, upon his release, could build a home for his victim's family and then build one for himself in the same "Reconciliation Village." We visited one of those villages in a small town named Mbyo, where we spoke with a woman whose whole family had been slaughtered. "For several years after the genocide the mere sight of a Hutu would make me vomit," she said, as Father Petero interpreted for her. "When I was approached by a representative of Prison Fellowship about the possibility of the man who had killed my family building me a house, I refused. There was no way I wanted anything to do with him. But I had no house, so eventually I reluctantly gave in, but I made it very clear that all I wanted was the house. However, while he was building my house, I soon got involved in helping him, handing him a tool or holding something in place. After a while I would also give him, first a drink of water, then a sandwich. Eventually, we became friends. Today, whenever I need something, he is on hand to help me, and I do the same for him." That whole village was composed of reconciled victims and perpetrators living together in peace. This is a model for the whole world.

We met Dativa, a remarkable young woman who was the director (warden) of the prison in the capital city of Kigali. She spent most of the day with us, telling us in great detail about their prison system and all that they did to rehabilitate people who had spent three months in 1994 slaughtering every member of the Tutsi tribe whom they could find. She herself was a survivor. Her entire family and most of her extended family had been killed. She summed up her prison philosophy by saying, "Because these people have committed such atrocious crimes, they need to be treated with a lot of love so they can be transformed."

That is the element that is missing in the prison system in the United States. There is nothing loving or transformative or forgiving about our system. On the contrary, it is all about primitive retaliation with no attempt at reconciliation. In fact, there is usually an order of protection issued preventing the perpetrator from ever contacting his victim's family, even to apologize. Our supposedly civilized system locks people up and abuses them, both physically and mentally, and turns them into angry monsters.

We invited Dativa to visit us at Sing Sing and gave her a grand tour. While gazing up at the five tiers of cages in B Block, she remarked, "It is appalling to see these people locked up in cages with nothing to do. It is no wonder that your prisoners have so many mental problems."

I had asked Javier to do a large painting to illustrate one of the talks I would be giving in the prisons. The painting was of Jacob's dream of a stairway between heaven and earth. At the bottom of the stairs were the fires of hell with people crying out in agony. Angels were reaching down from the stairway to lead them out of their misery so they could find their way to heaven. He completed the painting just before he was diagnosed with cancer. I did an inner healing meditation with the Rwandans about Jacob's dream, adapted from one I had done at one of our retreats at Sing Sing, inviting them to leave behind all of their hurts and injustices through forgiveness so they could proceed up the ladder to peace.

Before going to Rwanda, we had thought we were going there to share our expertise as prison chaplains and help them learn how to minister to prisoners more effectively. Instead, we were in awe of all that we learned from the people of Rwanda about the value of love and forgiveness in transforming criminals into responsible members of society. It was extremely humbling to see how effective this tiny, poverty-stricken country has been at accomplishing this goal. What a difference it could make in our own prison system if we could follow its example.

12

Fatherhood

Mother's Day is important in prison. The visiting room is always packed with mothers wanting to spend some time with their sons. In the weeks beforehand, Mother's Day cards are in great demand. One young fellow asked me for ten of them. When asked why he needed so many, he proudly replied, "One for each of my baby mamas." Although I was shocked by his pride in such an "accomplishment," I wasn't really surprised after hearing innumerable stories of the deadbeat, abusive fathers that had sired so many of the men. Like father, like son. Although the Mother's Day cards were hot items that disappeared as fast as I could replenish the stock, hardly anybody wanted Father's Day cards. There were a few hundred of them in the office when I arrived in 1995, and I still had some of them on hand when I left sixteen years later.

In counseling the men the biggest obstacle most of them had to overcome involved their relationship with their father. The damage that had been inflicted on them, whether by an abusive or a neglectful father, was catastrophic. While most of them adored their mothers, their attitude toward their fathers was resentful at best, but more often characterized by burning hatred. Those who had

had a healthy, loving relationship with their father were a distinct rarity in prison.

Resolving such a toxic relationship could not be brought about by simply telling them to forgive their fathers. How does one forgive a father who beat him, ridiculed him, and traumatized him for life? First, the person has to be able to recognize that what was done to him was terribly wrong and unjust. But even then, in many cases, it is impossible to repair the relationship. Some of their fathers were dead. Some were also in prison. Others were living lifestyles that were not conducive to a healthy relationship and were still abusive, miserable creatures. I often told the men that expecting a dysfunctional relationship to become normal would only drive them crazy. Sometimes, they simply had to let go of the relationship for the sake of their own sanity and move on. They didn't need to feel guilty for being unable to please an abusive father. It was their father's loss that he was unable and unworthy of having a relationship with them, and they were better off without him in their lives. Most important, I always stressed the need for them to break the cycle and not follow their father's example.

It was probably largely due to their lack of good fathering at home that so many of them looked to me as a surrogate father. Our chapel community became a therapeutic family, and I was the father of that family. In talking about me, many of my chapel members consistently referred to me as "the father." Very few of them had ever before had a positive male role model to care for them and give them some loving attention. But as their father, I also had to provide guidance and discipline to prevent our chapel family from becoming just as dysfunctional as their original one.

I did not like this role of disciplinarian, since that was supposed to be the role of the officers. But the discipline imposed by the officers was not done out of love but was itself often a form of abuse much like the abuse the men had experienced at home. The men needed someone who cared about them to teach them how to behave. They also needed a father figure to be their protector in the hostile environment of prison. Someone, for example, had to stand up to the drug dealers in the chapel and prevent them from destroying our family. Someone had to fight against discrimination and resolve disputes among the brethren whenever sibling-like rivalry created division.

Like all other fathers, I was not a perfect father and not always the ideal disciplinarian. There were moments when I would get quite annoyed by the day-to-day petty nonsense that was just as much a part of family life behind bars as it is in every other family. Sometimes certain manipulative individuals would push all the buttons until I would lose my temper. This was especially true when certain "wise guys" disrupted our Sunday mass. Being able to practice their religion was one of very few rights that had not been taken away from prisoners, and allowing them to worship freely without distractions or harassment was always my top priority. Anyone who interfered with that would quickly discover the wrath of God as pronounced by Father Ron.

On one occasion I saw a whole row of guys huddled together talking during my homily. My customary way of handling such a situation was to stop talking and glare at them until they got the message, much like any grade-school teacher would do. On this occasion, such subtlety was wasted. They were intently focused on something, and it definitely wasn't prayer. This went on throughout my whole homily, and I was getting steamed. So, at the end of my homily I stalked over to their pew and loudly demanded that they hand me their ID cards so I could give them a misbehavior ticket that would get them in trouble. One of the men, a middle-aged man named José, whom I had never seen before, asked in great astonishment if I wanted his, too. He was sitting in the same pew, so I presumed he was guilty and told him so.

After mass, before I had done anything about writing the men up, José indignantly informed me: "I just arrived at this facility this week. Upon coming to the chapel this morning, I sat down in that pew without knowing anybody. I could see that they were fooling around, but what could I do about it? I challenge you to tell me one single thing that I did that was inappropriate."

I could not swear that I actually had seen him doing anything. I had only seen him sitting in the same pew with those who were acting like buffoons and told him so.

José then responded, "I am greatly offended that you unjustly accused me of a crime that I did not commit. A judge and jury already did that to me, but for a priest to do the same thing is inexcusable, so you will never see me here again."

I immediately apologized to José and so as not to appear to be playing favorites I did not write any of them up. (Actually, in the sixteen years I worked there I only wrote up three people, and those were for much more serious offenses.) However, José refused to accept my apology and stormed out of the chapel. When I later went to see him in his cell, I again apologized, explaining, "I am a human being, and sometimes humans make mistakes. I was just hoping that you could find it in your heart to forgive me."

José was very polite. He told me that he had been in prison for a long time and had just come to Sing Sing for the college program. "I am not into any of that nonsense that was going on in the chapel. I appreciate your apology, but I want nothing more to do with organized religion. Please send me a 'Change of Religion' form so I can have the record show that I have no religion."

I was upset that I had hurt José so deeply and from then on prayed hard that he would have a change of heart.

Approximately one year later, when José was taking a speech class in the college program, one of the other students was acting up while he was trying to give a speech, and in his annoyance over the distraction he remembered the incident in the chapel. A few days later he saw me in the hallway and hollered: "Father Ron, I would like for you to call me over to the chapel to talk."

When he came to see me, he explained what had happened in the speech class and how annoyed he was about the distraction from a fellow student. "Now I understand why you were so annoyed with all the commotion that was going on in the chapel during your homily, and I just wanted to let you know that I am sorry for not having accepted your apology, and I am sorry for having turned my back on the chapel and on my faith."

I assured him that he was welcome back.

After that we became the best of friends, and he became an outstanding leader within the community and a great speaker at some of our retreats.

Sometimes my fatherly role was that of protector or mediator or intercessor. The sex offenders were extremely vulnerable and terrified for their lives whenever someone found out about their crime. I would calm them down and advise them on how to avoid problems, sometimes getting one of the more mature members of the community, such as José, to intercede on their behalf so that their tormentors would leave them alone. My main concern was always to make the chapel a safe haven, where everyone would feel protected.

But the most important role a father has in a family is to teach his sons how to become responsible fathers. Within our chapel family many of the men had never learned this skill from their original fathers, so as their surrogate father I had to assume that responsibility so that the cycle of abuse could be broken. Every year I devoted my Father's Day homily to helping these products of dysfunctional families learn how to become good fathers. Here is my homily from 2005:

Father's Day is a rough topic here in prison. Many of you have had abusive fathers. Some of you are fathers who have had no contact with your children in many years. So this holiday brings back a lot of painful memories. I could have focused this homily only on the scripture readings for today and gotten off easily. But the topic of fatherhood is extremely important, regardless of the kind of father you may have had or what your relationship with your children may be at the moment.

Those who were blessed with good fathers have much to be thankful for. Today is an opportunity to thank God for the gift of their love. But for those whose fathers left a lot to be desired, today is an opportunity to let go of past hurts and to try to forgive them for what they did or did not do. That is certainly not easy! But neither is the alternative—hanging on to past grudges and allowing them to cripple you with bottled-up anger and resentment. When that happens, you allow your fathers to continue to abuse you and thus prolong your misery. Once you can let go and forgive, you will be free, and they won't be able to hurt you anymore.

Coping with pain from the past can be frightening. Most prefer to bottle it up and try to forget about it. But that doesn't work. Sooner or later, repressed anger will surface and come out in very unpleasant and unhealthy ways. In today's Gospel, Jesus said not to be afraid. Of course, that is far easier said than done. But he has promised to help us cope with all our problems and to remain with us throughout the whole process.

But for now, this is enough said about our own fathers. Many of you are fathers yourselves. That too can be a painful subject and can bring up a lot of fears. Here, too, we need to allow Jesus to help us cope with whatever those fears may be.

Basically, one must recognize that there is far more to fatherhood than simply impregnating a woman and then leaving her with the responsibility of rearing that child all by herself. Some guys have requested as many as ten Mother's Day cards to give to the mothers of their various offspring scattered all over the country. I wish some of them *had* a little fear of the responsibility involved in being a father. Maybe that would help them keep their zippers up! They aren't loving, caring fathers. They are just irresponsible jerks.

Fatherhood is about responsibility—and you don't lose that responsibility when you come to prison. You can't change the past. But if you have fathered a child, you still have a responsibility to care for that child. Your present circumstances may limit your options considerably. I know some of you are not allowed to contact your children. Some of you might not even know where your children are. But you still have obligations to them that you can fulfill even in here.

The first of these obligations is to recognize that in most cases, you are the one who let your children down. It is not the fault of your children that you came to prison. Unless you are here unjustly, most likely it is your own fault that your family life got so complicated, so it is *your* responsibility to try as best you can to make amends for that. If your children want nothing to do with you right now, don't blame them or use that as an excuse to forget all about them. It may take many years before you can do anything to fix the problem, but file away in the back of your head that at some point before you die, you are the one who has to take the first step toward reconciliation.

The second thing you can do for your children in here is to pray for them. This is not just a pious cliche. Prayer is powerful! Even if your hands are temporarily tied by your present circumstances, God's hands are never tied, so call on God every day to intervene in your children's lives to help them cope with whatever problems they may be facing.

For those of you fortunate enough to still have contact with your children, write to them. Tell them you love them. Praise them for their accomplishments. Let them know you are proud of them. Those are things every child needs to hear—often. And if your children are too little to read, draw pictures to let them know you care. If possible, try to cooperate with their mother's attempts to correct them when they need it, but always do so out of love, never out of annoyance.

Being a father behind bars is not easy. But this is your God-given responsibility. To shirk that responsibility can have disastrous effects on your children's future and lead them to a place like this. That is why being a father is so frightening. Only a fool would not have a little fear about rearing children in today's complicated society. But God can help you overcome those fears so you can fulfill your responsibility. That is why your faith is so important. No matter how difficult the challenge may be, allow the Lord to give you the grace to overcome it, so you can be the kind of father your children deserve.

13

Life in Hell

The reason I often referred to the chapel as a "refuge in hell" was because prison is the closest thing to hell on earth. Every day, all day long, prisoners are subjected to dehumanizing and degrading abuse and persecution. The chapel was a safe place where they could come to escape the fires of hell and find refreshment. Those fires of hell came from many different sources.

Modern-day prison guards prefer to be called corrections officers or COs. Having spent four years working at West Point, where the most elite of the nation's army officers are trained, I was accustomed to officers being intelligent, respectful, respectable, and thoroughly professional. I met a few genuine officers at Sing Sing who fulfilled those qualifications. They were good people who performed their job in a professional manner, and I always had great respect for them. This chapter is not about them. Unfortunately, there were many who didn't even try to measure up to the most basic standards of professionalism or human decency and were a great embarrassment to the whole staff. Those officers who perform their duties in a professional manner know who they are. They also know the ones who are a disgrace to their uniform.

To qualify for a job as a CO, a candidate needs only a high-school diploma or GED plus seven weeks of training in the Department of Corrections Academy. Some can scarcely read and write English, as evidenced by the numerous tickets they write that are barely decipherable and consequently are inadmissible. In the army we had to pass a yearly physical fitness test, but some of these "officers" are grossly overweight and out of shape, which was certainly surprising in an environment where people's lives often depend on the COs' ability to quell violent disturbances.

When my clerk, Mark, became B Block's inmate grievance representative, his job required him to travel throughout all of the galleries of B Block to follow up on the grievances filed by various individuals against the prison staff. On one such occasion a new female CO, who was approximately five feet tall and over 250 pounds, asked him to do her a favor. She was unable to pull the brake that would mechanically open all of the cells on her gallery. (Because Sing Sing is such an old facility, the cells were locked and unlocked with an antiquated mechanical brake that was very difficult to operate.) Mark replied, "With all due respect, CO, you had better learn how to do this, because people's lives are at stake if you cannot open the cells." He then pulled the heavy brake to open the cells and tried to show her how to do it.

A little later she asked him to lock the cells, at which point he replied, "Excuse me, CO, but do you realize how much trouble I could get into if these guys see me lock them in their cells? I could be killed. You had better call one of the COs from the next gallery, because there is no fuckin' way I will ever lock somebody up. That is your job, not mine."

Many of the COs were extremely vulgar and foul-mouthed, with no sense of professional decorum. Although all of the New York State prisons are theoretically nonsmoking facilities, it was not unusual to see the COs lounging around smoking, even though they would not hesitate to write up a prisoner for doing so. Leading by example was definitely not one of their talents. Many of the COs at Sing Sing came from the same ghetto neighborhoods as the prisoners, and some still belonged to the same street gangs. The enormous number of drugs and weapons that were smuggled into Sing Sing on a daily basis would never have been possible without the cooperation of some of the COs. I always maintained that if they brought some drug-sniffing dogs to the line-up room at the beginning of each shift, the number of drugs getting into the facility would be drastically reduced. Similarly, one of those dogs in the visiting room would also make a huge difference.

Security is naturally a major concern in a maximum-security prison. But security should not be limited to preventing people from climbing over the wall to escape. It should be about the protection of every person inside those walls. Unfortunately, that kind of security never existed during the sixteen years that I worked at Sing Sing. Almost every day there were fights in which people were badly beaten or slashed by other prisoners. Where was the security then?

Even worse, certain rogue guards got their kicks out of beating people up. When questioned about it, they always claimed they were using "legitimate force" to quell a disturbance, but it was the same few who did this all the time and always got away with it.

One of my parishioners came into my office one day and showed me his T-shirt, covered with blood. A female guard had accused him of exposing himself in her presence. He had been in prison for many years and had never had any history of doing such a thing. The ticket had been immediately dismissed, rightly so, but the guard's boyfriend, a fellow CO, walked into his cell the following day and punched him in the nose, breaking it. He later filed a lawsuit against the state and against the guard and called me as a witness. Before the hearing, a representative of the attorney general's office tried to pressure me to change my testimony from the written report I had submitted at the time of the incident, claiming that it was impossible for such a thing to have happened. I refused. On an earlier occasion I had spoken with the deputy superintendent of security (DSS) about this particular guard and what a walking time bomb he was. The DSS acknowledged that he had had numerous complaints about the guard. But once the man resigned (before the hearing for his lawsuit), his personnel file was immediately "sanitized," so that when the investigators checked his record there were no longer any complaints on file, and, of course, the DSS could not recall our conversation.

I met a young man in the prison infirmary who had "fallen down the stairs" in his cell block. After staying in the infirmary for a few days he was told he would be returning to the block the following day, at which point he became hysterical. I couldn't understand what he was saying while he was yelling so hysterically in Spanish, but I reported his condition to the PSU. Unfortunately, it didn't do anything. That night he hung himself while the male guard who was supposed to be watching the unit was keeping company with the female nurse on duty in the nurses' station.

I later discovered that the fellow had been sharing a cell with a man who was repeatedly raping him. He had thrown himself down the stairs in an attempt to escape from his tormentor. When he was told he had to return to the man who was raping him, he thought it would be better to die. I reported all of this to the DSS, but according to his "investigation," no one was to blame for anything that happened.

On one of my regular visits to the Box, I walked in as two guards were dragging a semiconscious man into his cell. He had been severely beaten. Those two guards, incidentally, were into body building and looked as if they were pumped up on steroids, with their enormous biceps bulging in their tightly fitting sleeves. They also had extremely nasty dispositions. After beating the man up, they asked him in front of me if he wanted to go to the infirmary, but he said he would only go if I went with him. I wrote up the incident and was later called by the inspector general to testify in Albany about the situation, which I gladly did, much to the dismay of the superintendent. The officers were removed, and shortly thereafter cameras were installed in the Box. The New York State Corrections Officers' Union had been resisting their installation for years, but once they were installed there was a dramatic decrease in the number of people who were beaten up in that unit.

On one occasion when I was making rounds in the Box a man told me he couldn't take the abuse anymore and was going to "hang up." I immediately reported this to the mental-health social worker who was responsible for counseling the men in the Box. She laughed and said he was just trying to get attention and did nothing about it. A couple of days later he hung himself with his bed sheet. Fortunately, an alert officer was able to save his life, but that social worker should have been fired for such a callous attitude. Yet nothing happened to her.

A few months later there was a visit from the mental-health supervisors in Albany. They were meeting with the superintendent when I stopped by his office. When he introduced us, they asked if they could ask me a few questions about mental-health patients in the Box. Not wanting to speak in front of the superintendent, I replied that I was in a hurry and gave them my home telephone number. One of them called me a few days later, and I gave her an earful. I told her that being in the Box only made patients deteriorate even more, and then I described the incident mentioned above. I don't know if there was any connection between what I said and what happened later, but shortly thereafter that social worker was removed and new regulations were made prohibiting long-term Box sentences for mental-health patients.

The guards who worked the night shift were supposed to make regular rounds to make sure that all was well. Many, however, simply went to sleep. Others partied, and some had sexual liaisons, either with other guards or with prisoners. On one occasion a man got seriously ill during the night, vomiting profusely. When he called for the guard to help there was no answer, so he kept on calling. After a while the female guard's boyfriend (another guard), who was with her in her office, yelled for him to shut up or he would give him something to complain about. The man persisted, pleading that he was sick and needed to go to the infirmary. Eventually, two guards came to his cell and escorted him to the infirmary. According to the men in the surrounding cells, when he left his cell the man was walking. By the time he arrived at the infirmary, the prisoners who worked there as orderlies said he had been so severely beaten he was unable to walk. He was placed in a room by himself for the remainder of the night. When they checked on him the next morning he was dead.

RECIDIVISM

Regardless of a prisoner's offense, nobody is sentenced to a lifetime of abuse. The purpose of incarceration in a correctional facility is supposedly to correct a person's antisocial behavior. But when the people in charge of doing the correcting are corrupt, they turn it into a "corruptional" facility, making it hell on earth. That is why I have always referred to our state's Department of Corrections as the Department of Corruptions.

Most of the people who go to prison are there because of a variety of problems, most of which are related to addiction, mental-health issues, and childhood abuse. They are in need of treatment by skilled professionals who can help them change their ways. Unfortunately, that rarely happens, because most of the people treating them are neither skilled nor professional. Most people leave prison in worse shape than they were in before they arrived, which is why the recidivism rate is so deplorable.

The Daily Beast published an article titled "America's Recidivism Nightmare" by Caitlin Dickson on April 22, 2014. It cited the Bureau of Justice statistics on the rate of recidivism among 404,638 former state prisoners from thirty states who were released in 2005. "It found that 67.8 percent of them were re-arrested within three years of their release and 76.6 percent were re-arrested within five years." While a distinction must be made between arrests and convictions, such a high rate of re-arrests does not seem to indicate that our so-called correctional facilities are very effective in correcting criminal behavior.

Similarly, in March 2014 the Pell Center for International Relations and Public Policy published an article by Carolyn W. Deady titled "Incarceration and Recidivism: Lessons from Abroad." It states that "the United States has about 5% of the world's population yet it accounts for about 25% of the world's prisoners." Is this the mark of a civilized society? Deady went on to state that "the United States incarcerates more of its citizens than any other country—716 people per every 100,000, according to the International Centre for Prison Studies (ICPS)." In that same study the Russian Federation was in 10th place, Mexico in 67th place, the United Kingdom (England and Wales) in 102nd place, and Germany in 167th place. First place in such a competition is not the kind of rank we should brag about. Rather, we should hang our heads in shame.

The *New York Times* published an article on August 7, 2015, "What We Learned from German Prisons," from op-ed contributors Nicholas Turner and Jeremy Travis. They "led a delegation of people concerned about the United States criminal justice system to visit some prisons in Germany and observe their conditions." Their description of the conditions in German prisons was like comparing heaven to people living in hell, yet their system works. Ours doesn't. Turner and Travis observed: "But for all the signs of progress, truly transformative change in the United States will require us to fundamentally rethink values. How do we move from a system whose core value is retribution to one that prioritizes accountability and rehabilitation?"

From the moment a person is arrested, everything about our prison system is about punishment. Turner and Travis saw Germany's system as a potential model "premised on the protection of human dignity and the idea that the aim of incarceration is to prepare prisoners to lead socially responsible lives, free of crime, upon release." That is certainly not what happens in our New York State prison system.

Perhaps one of the reasons for such a striking difference is, according to the article, that "the process of training and hiring corrections officers is more demanding in Germany. Whereas the American corrections leaders in our delegation described labor shortages and training regimes of just a few months, in the German state of Mecklenburg–Western Pomerania, less than 10 percent of those who applied to be corrections officers from 2011 to 2015 were accepted to the two-year training program. This seems to produce results: In one prison we visited, there were no recorded assaults between inmates or on staff members from 2013 to 2014."

Such assaults occurred on a daily basis at Sing Sing as well as at numerous other New York prisons.

In the United States we often delude ourselves into thinking that our way is always the best way. Statistics, however, show that our prison system is not the most effective way of reforming criminals. If you lock a dog in a cage and torment and beat it every day, it will turn into a vicious animal. It is the same with people. Many prisoners already have serious anger issues from prior abuse. When they are abused by every element of the prison system throughout their incarceration, they become walking time bombs ready to explode. When that happens, they are beaten and isolated in the Box, where their inner turmoil and hatred continue to fester and grow steadily worse. Then they are released back to society. It is no wonder that so many prisoners keep coming back instead of being rehabilitated.

I do not mean to characterize all corrections officers in such a negative light. Sergeant Coop, for example, was a brightly shining star in this dismal setting. So was Sergeant Garder, who reported one of the male sergeants for throwing baby kittens into the trash compactor, for which he was fired and sent to jail. But numerous officers were supportive of the kitten killer at his trial, and many of them treated Sergeant Garder as a traitor and went out of their way to ostracize her. Many other COs were very helpful, both to me and to many of the prisoners, and performed their tasks in a professional manner. But as I said before, this chapter is not about them.

OTHER FORMS OF ABUSE

It was not just the COs who were abusive. The medical department for much of the time that I was there was a disgrace. With a few noble and notable exceptions, many of the nurses acted like agents of the Gestapo. In order to see a doctor, the men first had to see a sick-call nurse who more often than not would harshly interrogate them. The nurse would insinuate that they were lying about their symptoms and often turned them away without allowing them to get an appointment with a doctor. I know of numerous instances when the person was gravely ill and almost died because the sick-call nurse refused to believe he was telling the truth.

My worker Franco had frequent attacks of severe pain and vomiting. The nurse just gave him Pepto-Bismol and told him to stop complaining. This went on for months. I called the facility's medical director, who told me to mind my own business. Eventually Franco was admitted to the infirmary, but the doctor refused to do any diagnostic tests. I was with him when the doctor came to see him.

Franco asked why he didn't order any tests.

The doctor replied that he didn't think any were necessary.

Franco then asked him if he was just going to wait for him to die.

At this point the doctor started ranting and raving like a wild man, exclaiming, "Yes, that is exactly what I'm going to do. I'm going to stand here and wait for you to die!"

This was shouted loudly in the ward in front of a dozen other sick patients.

Then the doctor turned on me and started yelling at me for being there.

The guard on duty was furious with the doctor and told me to be sure to write him up, because he had almost caused a riot in the hospital. I wrote him up and this resulted in an investigation, and for once someone listened, because that doctor immediately disappeared.

About a year after the onset of his symptoms, Franco was finally sent to an outside hospital for tests that determined he was having kidney stone attacks.

Bobby had a sickly color to his face, no energy, and difficulty breathing. When I encouraged him to go to sick call, the nurse told him he was fine. It was obvious to anyone that he was far from fine. He could barely walk. So I suggested that he request emergency sick call during the night shift. The nurse who worked nights immediately recognized that there was something drastically wrong and called for an ambulance to take him to the outside hospital, where he was diagnosed with pneumonia. The doctor told him that if he had waited even a few hours longer he would have been dead.

That nurse was a true hero who bucked the system and did the right thing. When I thanked her profusely for helping Bobby, she replied: "I became a nurse to help people. That's what I do."

But soon afterward she left the prison in disgust because of the way nurses were so often prevented from showing any kind of care.

I know of two men who had what turned out to be appendicitis, but the sick-call nurse refused to believe that they were sick and sent them back to their cells after ridiculing them for pretending to be in pain when they were writhing in agony on the floor. In both cases the appendix ruptured, and they almost died, but nothing ever happened to the nurse. In the second of those cases, the prisoner submitted a formal complaint to the grievance committee. After an investigation, Albany determined that everyone had behaved "appropriately."

LACK OF CARE

When people are sentenced to do prison time, it is intended that their incarceration itself be their punishment. Being segregated from society and isolated from their families is indeed serious punishment. But it was never intended that any prisoner be sentenced to sadistic torture and further injustices such as those that occurred on a regular basis in Sing Sing. While prisoners are incarcerated, the prison is responsible for providing "care, custody and control," according to the mission statement. The prison fulfilled its responsibility of custody and control reasonably well in that escapes and riots were rare. The care aspect, however, was seriously lacking. It was lacking on the part of administrators who tolerated abuses in every area of the prison. It was lacking in Albany, where aloof bureaucrats appointed incompetent administrators who perpetuated the problem.

Another area where care was lacking was in nutrition. Albany allotted $1.37 per prisoner per meal for food when I first arrived there in 1995. The same amount is allotted as of this writing. Since the price of food has steadily risen, that means the quality and quantity have steadily declined. It was a very unhealthy diet in 1995, based primarily on starch. Salads consisted of limp, semi-spoiled greens with a few stale shreds of carrots and cabbage. The use of margarine added deadly trans fats.

But at least in the 1980s and even into the 1990s food was prepared from scratch by the mess hall workers, which provided excellent training for them in all aspects of food preparation and service as well as ensuring the food's freshness. Now, however, everything is prepared elsewhere and shipped in "quick chill" plastic bags, which often sit for days in the cooler before being used.

The selections—as they appeared on the printed menu—often seemed quite appetizing. For example, the menu for Thanksgiving was usually

> Roast Tom Turkey with Stuffing and Gravy
> Candied Yams and Cranberry Sauce
> Garden Salad
> Pumpkin Pie

However, since I was always there on holidays, I often stopped by the units to visit prisoners who were confined to their cells, in the Box, and in the hospital, so I saw the actual meals that were delivered. On the plate was a slice of processed turkey loaf with canned gravy and stuffing that had the consistency of a hockey puck. The candied yams were not really candied but straight out of a can, just like the cranberry sauce. The salad was barely edible. The only thing worth eating was the pumpkin pie. Most of the other meals were far worse and have gotten steadily worse every year.

Employees are theoretically not allowed to eat state food. But at Sing Sing it was common practice for the guards to eat what was intended for the prisoners because they were too cheap to bring their own lunch to work. While the prisoners weren't allowed additional portions of anything, the guards helped themselves to as much as they wanted, thus reducing the amount available for the prisoners. With the hundreds of guards who ate there every day (without charge), that meant a substantial decrease in the already meager food allotment. When the commissioner of corrections attended one of our chaplains' retreats, I brought this problem to his attention, but he sarcastically suggested that the chaplains all take a pay cut to offset the cost of improving the prisoners' diet.

All of the prisoners are given meager wages, usually between three and five dollars per week, depending on their job assignment. Those wages have not been increased in decades, but the cost of all of the items in the prison commissary has steadily risen, so the number of items they can purchase has greatly decreased. With a steadily deteriorating diet and a decreasing ability to purchase supplementary items from the commissary, the public perception of prisoners living a life of luxury is far from accurate. Unless they have outside support from family or friends, they lose a lot of weight on their meager subsistence diet. Only the ones with outside support can afford the extra calories needed to work out and build up their physique.

There is another form of abuse that comes from chaplains. I have heard scandalous stories about some of the chaplains in other facilities who don't care about anyone or anything except their paycheck. Some wouldn't even provide a cup of coffee for their workers. Many of them relate better to the abusive guards than to the people to whom they are supposed to be ministering.

Occasionally I contacted a chaplain to let him know a man who had been in my religious education class had been transferred to his facility only to be told that he didn't have time to offer any religious education classes. One Catholic chaplain actually told Catholic prisoners that if they wanted religious instructions they should go to the Protestants. A large number of African priests are becoming chaplains. Some of them have such heavy accents that no one can understand them. There are numerous chaplains of all religious persuasions who have no work ethic and are "missing in action" more than they are present.

We were truly blessed at Sing Sing by having full-time Protestant, Catholic, and Muslim chaplains who worked well together to collectively serve the needs of all the prisoners regardless of their faith, and we actually enjoyed one another and socialized together. All three of us went to Rwanda, although not all at the same time because someone had to stay behind to take care of the prisoners. But I knew of numerous facilities where the chaplains of different faiths didn't even speak to one another. They seemed to think that they were in competition instead of working together to minister to the needs of the prisoners. Even worse, they often were more interested in "brown nosing" the administration than in caring for their parishioners.

Caring for prisoners is about as popular as caring for black people in the Jim Crow days of the South or for Jews in Nazi Germany. Prisoners have been relegated almost to a non-person status, while the general public has been brainwashed into thinking they are living overly pampered lives at the taxpayers' expense. Myths abound about their lavish medical and dental care, which in fact is not only difficult to access but usually substandard. People complain about their access to television, for which they must pay an overly inflated price out of their meager earnings for a tiny black-and-white set if they want one in their cell, with only basic channels available. A chaplain's role is to advocate for the prisoners, but advocating is rarely appreciated, and my attempts were not without reprisals. Caring people are not welcome in prisons. They are a threat to the status quo. Throughout my time at Sing Sing, my attitude continually got me in trouble.

THE COST OF CARING

The first time my job was threatened was early in my career. One of my parishioners asked me to tell the DSS about a plan he had overheard. A man had been badly beaten by two guards who were notorious for doing such things, but to justify their actions they had claimed that he had attacked them. This was an additional crime, for which he had seven years added to his sentence. The man who was beaten, however, was a member of a gang, and he had found out the guards' home addresses and had made arrangements for gang members on the outside to execute both of them as well as their families. Although nobody had any great love for either of the two guards, my parishioner did not want their family members slaughtered, which was why he had asked me to intervene.

The DSS investigated the situation and discovered evidence that the threat was real, and steps were taken to prevent the executions from happening.

Everything turned out well, except that my immediate supervisor, the DSP, was quite upset that I had not informed him about it first. I let him know that this had been told me in confidence and that I was asked to speak only to the DSS, but he was adamant that I was supposed to follow the proper chain of command, beginning with him. I told him I would never violate a confidence, at which point he brought in the union representative and threatened to fire me. I told him he could fire me, but that I would sue his pants off.

Later I explained my predicament to the prisoner who had started the whole thing, and he wrote a letter to Cardinal O'Connor, explaining that I could not defend myself in this area because I could not violate his confession. The cardinal sent a representative to speak with the commissioner in Albany, and the DSP was transferred.

Another occasion when my job was threatened involved providing financial assistance to prisoners. There are strict rules preventing state employees from doing almost anything to help a prisoner, and most of those rules are necessary, as shown in the 2015 escape from the Clinton Correctional Facility, a maximum-security prison in upstate New York. However, if I followed all of the rules in the handbook, I would never get anything done. I was there to help people, and I did so in many different ways for the whole time I worked there. As long as I knew that it was a legitimate need, I didn't allow the rules to get in the way of helping. In some cases it was a simple phone call to a relative that I would make from home for a man in the Box, or I would give a postage stamp to someone who wanted to write home. When George had become incontinent after prostate surgery, I provided him with diapers because the infirmary refused to do so. I gave newcomers deodorant and other toiletries. When someone with AIDS needed yogurt to counteract the effect of his medications, I brought some in, since neither the infirmary nor the mess hall would provide it. When people needed to pay for tuition for the college program, I made arrangements from the outside to pay for it. If I had asked permission to do any of these things, the answer would have been no, so I never asked.

On one occasion a check from My Father's House that I had sent to pay for a man's correspondence course was unexpectedly returned to the facility, since I had used the prisoner's return address instead of my own. That got me into trouble, and the superintendent immediately turned the matter over to the inspector general for an investigation. They wanted to know if I had been coerced into paying it or if I was paying for sexual favors, to which I replied, "Absolutely not!" I did not volunteer the information that I had been doing this for years, but I explained that it was for a parishioner who was very involved in our chapel, and I simply wanted to help him. I was almost fired, but fortunately the archdiocese was able to plead my case and, after a year of haggling, my job was spared, much to the dismay of our superintendent.

INCOMPETENT ADMINISTRATORS

The only reason the guards were able to get away with such un-professional conduct was because of incompetent administrators. They spent most of the day in their comfortable offices but spent minimal time seeing what was actually going on, especially during the evening and night shifts. Once they left for the day, the prison was essentially run by the guards, who did whatever they wanted, regardless of what they were supposed to be doing. Even when the superintendent and other members of the Exec Team made weekly rounds, the guards would always phone ahead so everybody along the route would be awake and on their best behavior. Like the guards, most of the administrators had minimal training for their responsibilities. Many of them simply worked their way up from the bottom. In that particular environment the common sentiment was that "scum rises." Good, intelligent people were often passed over for promotions that were given to people who were incompetent and corrupt.

LACK OF PREPARATION FOR REENTRY TO SOCIETY

When the Department of Corrections annexed the Division of Parole, it changed its name to Department of Corrections and Community Supervision, and it made a big deal out of how it was now making great strides to prepare prisoners for their return to society. The counselors were now responsible for doing the work of the former facility parole officers in addition to their own. They greatly resented these additions to their workload and were poorly trained for them. Yet the transition of released prisoners back into the community is in their reluctant hands, and some of them botch the job badly.

I discovered this firsthand after my retirement when attempting to arrange for a prisoner named Joe to be released to a rehab before I would allow him to come to My Father's House. I had contacted St. Joseph's Rehabilitation Center in Saranac Lake, run by the Graymoor Franciscan Friars of the Atonement, who told me they would need to conduct an intake interview with him over the telephone before he was released.

Joe first contacted his counselor/facility parole officer, who ignored his request. He then wrote to his counselor's supervisor, who also ignored his request. Finally, I called the DSP and explained the whole situation to her. She thanked me for my interest and told me she would take care of it if I sent her some information about the rehab. I emailed the information to her state email address, but it was the wrong address. I called again, and she didn't know her own email address and had to get it from the secretary. I sent the information again. A week later nothing had been done. This was just three weeks before his scheduled release. I called her back, and she was unaware that I had sent her the information. When she finally found the email, she assured me he would be able to have the interview, but it never happened. Then I contacted her supervisor in Albany, who said he didn't want to interfere with anything that the DSP was doing. The end result was that the man, who recognized his need for a drug rehab and was voluntarily requesting to go to one, was unable to get the help he needed, because nobody in the facility wanted to do his or her job.

In this case the prisoner fortunately was able to be released to his sister's address, but time after time, these counselors/parole officers wait until the very last minute to seek approval for a proposed housing or rehab request. When the slightest problem occurs, the soon-to-be-released prisoner might find out the day before his release that his housing request with his mother or other family member has been denied, so that he has to be released to a shelter. Meanwhile, Joe, who was unable to get the help he needed, relapsed and ended up back in prison. This is the "community supervision" aspect of corrections in action at the taxpayers' expense.

This gross lack of preparation for reentry into society is the most insidious form of abuse, because it guarantees that the majority of the former prisoners will return to prison. Over the years I became convinced that Father Donovan, the elderly chaplain from Green Haven Correctional Facility, who mentored me in the beginning of my career, was correct in his assertion that the prison system was run by an "evil empire" that had created the very lucrative "prison industrial complex."

That is not to say that everyone who works for the prison system is evil, but there is something intrinsically evil about the system itself. It is the only business in the world that makes money by turning out a bad product. If it were to succeed in its stated goal of rehabilitating people before returning them to society, that would be bad for business. So, the Parole Boards keep on hitting those with violent offenses with two more years, since they know that the so-called violent offenders are the least likely to reoffend. But while the maximum-security prisons are bulging at the seams, the medium-security prisons are far from full. I believe that is why they do everything possible to prevent the drug addicts from getting the treatment they need—so they will keep coming back.

Much criticism has been given to private contractors who run prisons for profit, and rightly so. But the state prison system is just as corrupt and has just as many contractors who are treating the entire prison system as the "goose that lays the golden egg," beginning in Albany and trickling all the way down to the local facilities. All levels of management are making too many millions of taxpayers' dollars to risk a reduction in clientele, which is why

I believe they deliberately go out of their way to make sure that most of the prisoners they release will come back to prison. The numerous prisons in the upstate counties of New York are a huge boon to their respective economies, and nobody wants to close any of them, because that would put people out of work and have a negative ripple effect. Shortly after Governor Andrew Cuomo was elected, he visited Tryon Residential Facility for Youth. It had no prisoners in it. Yet the staff continued to come to work every day, do their jobs, collect a paycheck, and use heat and electricity at an empty prison. Needless to say, he closed it, along with numerous other facilities that were no longer needed.

When prisoners are released, they usually have nothing more than forty dollars in their pocket, the clothing on their back, and no place to go. Many of them are assigned to a drug rehab, but many of those rehabs are unfit for human habitation.

Angel was in and out of prison for most of his adult life because of drug addiction. He had no trouble staying clean in prison, but every time he was released he was forced to go to either a shelter or a rehab. It was difficult to say which was worse. In the shelter he was robbed and lived in fear for his life. In the latest rehab to which he was sent, he was covered with bedbug bites after his first night of "freedom."

Since most rehabs make their money according to the number of beds that are filled, they try to run at full capacity. Although they have rules forbidding the use of drugs and alcohol, residents quickly discover that those rules are rarely enforced. In some cases even the so-called drug counselors are active users. But many of the newly released prisoners are forced by their parole officer to be in those drug-infested "rehabs" which almost guarantee that they will return to drugs and to prison. These rehabs are just one more way of ripping off taxpayers and preventing the newly released prisoners from getting the help they need to rebuild their lives. It is not surprising that the drug rehabs and shelters keep the prison industrial complex flourishing.

COPING WITH ABUSE

Dealing with such mistreatment on a daily basis can be extremely frustrating, so I had to develop a strategy for coping with it. Seething and fuming only made me miserable. What worked best for me was the realization that the prison was a mission field. I was continually inspired by the Maryknoll missioners, whose worldwide mission headquarters was up the hill from Sing Sing. Many of them have faced horrendous persecution and even martyrdom in hostile territories like China, El Salvador, and Guatemala for the sole crime of daring to proclaim liberty to captives. They went to those countries to defend the rights of the poor, who were often greatly oppressed by corrupt, tyrannical governments. The tyranny I faced at Sing Sing was annoying and frustrating, but it was nothing compared to what other missionaries have had to endure. It was just part of the price that needed to be paid for the privilege of ministering to prisoners. But there were moments when I had to grit my teeth and pray hard not to open my mouth when dealing with the sheer lunacy, religious bigotry, and deliberate persecution that occurred there on a daily basis.

14

Farewell

Coping with so much abuse and injustice on a daily basis took a toll on me. The stress got to be unbearable at times. While there were many occasions when I thought about retiring, I could never abandon my flock. I very much identified with Saint John as he stood at the foot of the cross witnessing the most horrible injustice imaginable. He would have given anything to be able to pull the nails out of the hands and feet of his Lord and take him off of that instrument of torture, but he was powerless to do anything. But he was there—and his loving presence was surely a great comfort to Jesus in his dying moments. In my chapel there were lots of men hanging in agony on the crosses designed for them by the "Department of Corruptions," and there was often little I could do to combat the gross injustices that, in some cases, had put them there. But as long as I was with them, they knew that somebody loved them and that somebody cared.

Besides that, I really enjoyed my work in that "garbage can," helping people our society had discarded. But at the same time I had the feeling that God had something else in store for me, although I didn't know what that might be. One day in the spring of 2011 in my daily prayers I told the Lord that if he ever wanted me to leave Sing Sing He would have to make it very clear to me because I loved my chapel community too much to leave it of my own free will. The very next day the headlines of the local paper stated that pressure was being placed on the governor to close Sing Sing. I knew then that God knew how to get my attention, and that helped prepare me for what was to come next.

I had been invited by my friend Father Petero, with whom I had gone to Rwanda, to give a three-day seminar on prison ministry at a seminary in Haiti in July. On the Friday afternoon before we left, I received a phone call from the archdiocese saying that the commissioner no longer wanted me working at Sing Sing due to my "inappropriate relationships" with the prisoners. I was stunned! The priest from the archdiocese had no more details and asked me what I could have done that was so inappropriate. I had no idea. I informed him I was leaving on Monday for Haiti and would talk to him upon my return.

The seminar in Haiti went well. I told the seminarians about our retreats in Sing Sing and Bedford Hills and how the prisoners shared their witness stories. We then helped them prepare a seminar at the prison in Port-au-Prince. Since I knew we wouldn't have time to help the Haitian prisoners prepare witness talks, I brought with me talks given by the women at Bedford Hills on their recent retreat. The seminarians then translated them into French for use in the prison. Dativa, the former warden from the prison in Rwanda who had visited Sing Sing, was then working for the United Nations to oversee the prisons of Haiti, and it had been at her invitation that we had gone there. She gave us a guided tour through the women's prison and introduced the seminarians to the prison officials to make the proper connections for conducting a retreat in the future. It was nice to see Dativa again, and she hosted a lovely party in her spacious home, introducing us to their commissioner of corrections, with whom we had a lively conversation.

But the whole time I was there, my mind was churning. What were these "inappropriate relationships" that the commissioner was talking about? In the middle of my third sleepless night it suddenly occurred to me. He must have found out about my letter writing.

While working at the county jail in 1994–95, I began corresponding with numerous people I had counseled after they were sentenced and transferred to the state prison system as a means of providing ongoing spiritual support and encouragement. Once I transferred to Sing Sing, I didn't want to abandon them, so I continued to write for several years until there was a crackdown from on high, and I was told not to write to anyone. I stopped writing for a few months, but they continued writing to me and asked why I had abandoned them. For some of them, I was the only person on earth who cared whether they were dead or alive. Many of them had been suicidal, and I had encouraged them to keep on living. As a result, I started writing to them under a fictitious name and address. In some cases I used their name but added "Sr." after it, posing as their father, as in John Smith, Sr. In other cases I used the names of friends and used their return addresses. Since the facility normally only checks incoming mail, they were able to continue to write directly to me. Over the years my correspondence list grew tremendously as I continued to stay in touch, not only with the ones from the county jail, but those from Sing Sing who had been transferred elsewhere.

During the ten years that I corresponded with Barney, a middle-aged army veteran, his wife left him. Then his grandmother, aunt, and uncle died. His ex-wife was declared an unfit mother, so his young son was taken away from her and put in foster care and later adopted. Then two of his sisters died of drug overdoses, his mother died from cancer, and his son's new mother dropped dead of a heart attack in front of him. Meanwhile, Barney almost died twice from medical complications. Throughout all of this I was all he had to keep him going. Somehow, I surmised, the commissioner, with whom I had locked horns on numerous occasions, must have found out about my letter writing.

At that point I had to make a decision. The archdiocese had offered to fight on my behalf, as it had done several times in the past, but those fights usually dragged on for many months. What I was most afraid of was that the inspector general would start investigating the men with whom I had corresponded. Those investigations rarely turned out well, because the investigators always presumed that the prisoners were lying and treated them accordingly.

This administration never played fair and could be very retaliatory. It had already tried to get me fired over trivial nonsense, even while guards continued to smuggle in drugs and prostitute themselves with impunity. I knew that sooner or later it would get me, so there in Haiti, in the middle of the night, I made the heart-wrenching decision to bow out gracefully and retire, even though it broke my heart.

When I returned home at the end of the week I informed the archdiocese of my decision, but I decided to wait until after the weekend to inform the prison. On Saturday evening I went to the chapel and told my workers, then returned for mass on Sunday morning. Nobody except my chapel workers knew what was going on, so we proceeded with mass as usual. At the end of my brief homily I said, "That was the easy part; now here comes the hard part." Then through many tears I explained exactly what had transpired and that I would be resigning that week but wanted to say goodbye and let them know how much I had enjoyed working with them. At the end of the mass I invited anyone who was so inclined to come up to the microphone and speak. Almost everyone in the chapel did so. Many of them were in tears as they told everyone how much I had meant to them and how I had helped them to change their lives. They all hugged me. It was a real love feast and was truly one of the most powerful experiences of love I have ever known. Then I went over to Bedford Hills and did the same thing with the women. Once again, there were lots of tears and hugs and broken hearts.

My resignation was to go into effect on September 2, 2011, to use up my remaining vacation days. I was hoping to continue to come in while on vacation, but Albany made it clear that I could not enter either facility during that time. I was afraid to continue to write to anyone, because I knew there would be a big investigation and didn't want to cause the men any trouble. So, for two months I sat at home alone, in great despair, wondering if life was worth living without my beloved family behind bars.

I knew I needed help and started seeing a psychologist. I told him, "I feel like my entire family has been wiped out in a plane crash. My whole identity is gone. I used to be the chaplain at Sing Sing Prison, but all of a sudden I feel like I am nobody." I wrote a letter to Cardinal Dolan apologizing for letting him and the prisoners down. I actually intended it to be a farewell letter as I contemplated suicide, but through the loving support of friends I was able to regain my senses enough to resist that urge. I requested and was granted some time off from the archdiocese, because I knew I could not function in any kind of ministerial capacity when I was falling apart.

The same day that my resignation was official I resumed writing to my prison family, explaining the whole situation. Suddenly, my correspondence list multiplied. In addition to all the men in other prisons throughout the state with whom I had been corresponding,

I now had another list of parishioners at Sing Sing and at Bedford Hills who were as anxious to hear about me as I was to hear about them. At their request I began sending them copies of my homilies and also developed a Prisoners' Correspondence Course from the classes I had given.

Once I began hearing from the men in other prisons, I discovered that only one of them had been interrogated by the inspector general about me. That was Mark, who had been in charge of our ministry of hospitality until he was transferred to another prison. When the inspector general asked him what he could tell him about me, Mark replied, "You have dirty cops in here selling drugs and prostituting themselves on a daily basis, and you are worried about Father Ron? You are investigating the wrong man. Everybody in the whole state knows that he is the only person who gives a damn about prisoners, so fuck you. I have nothing more to say to you." That was the end of the interview.

A few of the men from the chapel at Sing Sing were interrogated, but there was no dirt to be found, so the investigation went nowhere. If they had found anything during the two months before my retirement went into effect they could have fired me. Instead, I simply retired a little sooner than I would have liked, but with a pension from the state.

I tortured myself for a while with "if onlys," but eventually I came to the realization that this was God's way of letting me know my work there was done.

Another chapter of my life is already under way as a hospital chaplain and as one of the founders of Catholic Whistleblowers, a support group for people like me who blew the whistle on the clergy sex-abuse problem, and working with Voice of the Faithful in providing Restorative Justice Healing Circles for the survivors of clergy sex abuse. I also remain in close contact with my family behind bars through letter writing and phone calls.

The only thing that remains now from my previous chapter at Sing Sing is to tell the story on behalf of my wonderful family behind bars. This is their story, too, that I promised to share with the outside world, and we all thank you for listening.

Testimonials from Behind Bars

I asked Steve, the Jewish chapel clerk, and some of the other men mentioned in the book to write about the impact that my ministry had upon their lives.

Steve

I was incarcerated at Sing Sing Correctional Facility for approximately eleven of the sixteen years that Father Ron spent as the Catholic chaplain there. To me, he was a bright shining light in an otherwise dismal and gloomy setting. Although I am not Catholic, through the years I enjoyed the distinct pleasure of attending many services and events at the Catholic chapel, particularly at Christmas and Easter. Moreover, whenever I or hundreds of other men not of the Catholic faith were in need of assistance, rather than speak to the clergy representing our own persuasion, we would invariably seek out Father Ron; he was always more responsive and helpful.

Father Ron's book is an honest and objective inside view of the realities and frustrations of prisoners, the vast majority of whom, prior to their incarceration, lived in impoverished neighborhoods suffused with illegal drug addiction and alcohol abuse. Indeed, warehousing such individuals for a protracted period of years and then returning them to their old neighborhoods is a guaranteed prescription for recidivism. Further, many first-offenders, after graduating from their frustrating prison experience, return to the streets as hardened and infinitely more experienced criminals.

This deeply moving book, filled with stories of actual people and events, is a chronicle of convicted persons at the mercy of life and the prison system. When I read the manuscript for this book, I was filled with both the urge to weep and the urge to roar. The message of this memoir is that in the midst of all the misery and degradation, there is hope. If someone, in this case a dedicated Catholic priest, is willing to provide a measure of understanding, it could very well mean the difference between failure and salvation.

I found reading this manuscript to be a challenging and deeply moving experience. Father Ron's message deserves to be read carefully, slowly, thoughtfully, and repeatedly. It is also a testament to the power of spiritual life, which will appeal even to those who have no interest in religion.

This manuscript is a great reminder, if not exposé, of what awaits anyone who is swallowed up and deposited into the bowels of the criminal justice system. *Refuge in Hell* should be required reading for every prison administrator and corrections officer throughout the United States to remind them that men and women are sent to prison *as* punishment, and not *for* punishment.

Mark

I was Father Ron's minister of hospitality for two years at Our Lady of Hope Chapel in Sing Sing. Although he describes me as having an outgoing personality and as being the life of the party, on the inside I was a tormented soul, plagued by demons of addiction and filled with guilt and remorse. My time at Sing Sing was truly a walk through the "valley of the shadow of death," and I thank God that

Father Ron was with me on that scary journey. Working for him in the chapel was the only thing that helped me find peace and sanity.

Father Ron's love for prisoners was amazing. We had done some really awful things to other people, but he never judged us and always tried to help us face our problems and rebuild our lives. As a chapel worker I was lucky to be able steal a lot more of his undivided time and attention, even when I was still on a self-destructive mission. Even while working for him, there were times when I still gave in to temptation and got high, running up a drug debt that could have cost me my life. But when I told Father Ron about it, he paid the debt. Although I lost my job in the chapel, he never gave up on me and kept on trying to help me change my ways. His patient guidance stayed with me long after I left Sing Sing. His letters and homilies helped me to stay on course.

I consider myself to be one of God's chosen ones to have been blessed by my relationship with Father Ron while in the midst of the madness that is the "Department of Corruptions," as he describes the government agency. I am also hoping to be one of his success stories; I have been free from drugs for the past ten years. The prison system didn't help me accomplish that. It was the grace of God and the patient, loving guidance that I received from Father Ron in the special refuge that he created for us in Sing Sing.

Johnny

Words could never describe how thankful I am for Father Ron because of all he has done for me. In a nutshell, he saved my life, and it all started in the safe refuge that he maintained in Sing Sing. I had been badly abused as a child and was filled with rage. I never listened to anybody and was not capable of reaching out for help. Following in my father's footsteps I became an alcoholic, and addiction took over my life at an early age. Instead of recognizing that something was wrong with me, I blamed everyone else for all my problems. I surrounded myself with equally disturbed people, one of whom became my girlfriend. That dysfunctional relationship was a recipe for disaster. We fought constantly. Our fighting, fueled by alcohol and drugs, eventually led to violence and a sentence of ten years. At that point I thought my life was over, and I was petrified.

In the county jail I prayed for the first time in many years and begged God to help me. Now I know God answered that prayer. The first prison I arrived at was Sing Sing. My first Sunday there I went to the Catholic chapel. After leaving my filthy, noisy cellblock filled with abusive officers and dangerous inmates, I entered a chapel that looked like it had dropped out of heaven. People welcomed me. The atmosphere was filled with joy, and I felt at peace. This was the first time I saw Father Ron. It seemed like he was speaking directly to me in his homily, as if he knew my whole situation. To my embarrassment, tears began streaming down my cheeks. I went for the next few weeks, and the same thing kept happening. He would give his homily, and I would fight hard to hold back my tears.

One day Father Ron stopped me and asked if we could talk. He wanted to know what I had done to end up in prison, and how I was doing. He was never judgmental, and I found it easy to talk to him. Our conversation ended with him inviting me to choir practice. I couldn't believe it. I had never sung in my life, but I said I would give it a try. Much to my amazement, I enjoyed it. I went to every mass, choir practice, and class he had, and at least once a week he called me to the chapel during the day so we could talk at length. One day he said: "Johnny, I know you are hurting inside. We need to get that out so your past can't haunt you anymore." In spite of my trepidation I began opening up about my abusive childhood. He patiently helped me work through all those issues. The more we talked, the better I felt. This was what I had needed my whole life.

After a year, when I had to leave Sing Sing for another jail, I was heartbroken. But Father Ron pulled me aside and said: "I don't usually do this, but I believe in you. You have come a long way, but we still have some work to do." He gave me his home address and told me to write to him. I have been writing to him ever since. Once he retired, I put him on my phone list, and we talk almost every day. I eventually let go of my abusive biological father and cut all ties with the rest of my dysfunctional family, since they had been one of the major causes of stress all my life, and because they had abandoned me in prison. Once I did this, I felt free, and this enabled me to grow tremendously.

I've learned from Father Ron to never let my past abuse define who I am today. I am a survivor, not a victim. From the beginning of our relationship he offered hope, courage, and love. His ongoing presence in my life has given me the strength to overcome all of my trials. He is the only father figure I've ever had. Through his loving guidance, this man not only changed my life, but has given me a new life. When I was praying in the county jail, I had no idea how God would answer my prayers. But today I know that it is by the grace of God that Father Ron came into my life so that I could become the person that I am today.

Pat

"I've been waiting two years to meet you." This was the greeting that welcomed me to the Westchester County Jail the day after my conviction for manslaughter. The words were spoken by a priest with a black beard and expressive eyes. His voice was calming and reassuring. Little did I know the role this man would play in my life over the next two decades.

The words he spoke to me through bars of steel were comforting. He was a man who wanted to get to know me. He wanted to meet the person who had committed the horrible crime he had heard about in the news. He asked me if I would like to talk to him. When I agreed, a guard opened my cell, and Father Ron brought me to a room where we could talk in private. He did not condemn me as a criminal. As Jesus forgave the thief on the cross, Father Ron let me know that Jesus would forgive me, too. After we talked a while, Father Ron asked if I would like to go to confession. I would, indeed. As I confessed my crime, the pressure inside of me lessened, as if Father Ron had absorbed all the guilt bottled up inside of me for so many years. When we finished, Father Ron asked if he could hug me. As his arms wrapped around me, I felt welcomed into a flock with the protection of a shepherd. From then on, each time I see him we welcome each other with a hug.

After a few months at the county jail I was due to be sentenced. I was nervous, not because of the amount of time I was expecting, but because the family of my victims would have the opportunity to express the pain, anguish, anger, and sorrow I had caused them. When I talked to Father Ron about this, he assured me that he would be in the courtroom to offer his support, and he volunteered to speak on my behalf if it would be permitted.

Father Ron's presence at the sentencing was a great consolation as I listened to the anguished cries of the family members telling the court how badly I had hurt them. But when their statements were over, the judge asked Father Ron to come to the podium. As he spoke, I knew that he saw me for the man that I really am, not the image portrayed by my actions at one point in time. At that moment I knew this was a man who had a calling to lead a flock of felons.

Two months after my sentencing I was transferred into the New York State prison system and three months later arrived at Sing Sing. When I asked about the Catholic chapel I was told that they were between priests and services were held on a sporadic basis. When I finally made it to a service, my spirit lifted as I saw Father Ron. He greeted me with his signature hug.

When Father Ron and I talked after mass, he told me he was running into bureaucratic hassles delaying his full-time appointment as chaplain. I asked my wife to contact a reporter we knew at the local newspaper. The reporter then wrote a column asking why there was such a delay. Within a few weeks, the red tape holding Father Ron back from his calling disappeared. He inherited a parish that was in a state of neglect. The chapel was in disrepair, and the flock of Catholics was scattered. Father Ron asked the administration if I could be assigned as his clerk, but once his supervisor learned that he knew me from the county jail, I was immediately transferred.

Thus began my journey through four other correctional facilities over the next fifteen years. During that time I stayed connected to the Catholic Church in each facility. However, it was never the same. Something was always missing from the priests or deacons there. My saving grace was my correspondence with Father Ron. Through his letters he continued to give me the spiritual support and counsel I needed. When he sent me his homilies in the mail, it was as if he was speaking directly to me in my cell.

Throughout my incarceration I longed to be in the presence of my shepherd once again. That happened in 2009 when I volunteered to return to Sing Sing to enroll in the master's degree program offered there by New York Theological Seminary. The second morning that I awoke back at Sing Sing, it was to the voice of a now gray-bearded Father Ron welcoming me back. Although he could not reach me to hug me through the bars of my cell, his eyes and words comforted me. Later that morning I was able to go to the chapel. What I saw amazed me. Gone were the dingy and dilapidated conditions I had seen years earlier. The chapel was magnificent. Father Ron had breathed new life, not only into the physical structure, but also into the spirituality of the men who attended Our Lady of Hope. The whole chapel was revitalized. This was evident in the schedule of programs and the number of volunteers who came from the local community to share their faith with us.

The majority of my time at Sing Sing was filled with school and studying. However, I always made time to be a part of the Catholic community. When my graduation finally arrived in May 2010, my family was able to attend for an evening of celebration. One of my fondest mementos from that night is a picture taken with my family: my parents, my wife and children, my siblings, and Father Ron. I know that no matter where I go, imprisoned or free, Father Ron will always be a part of my family. Someday I will be able to spend time with him on the outside; however, until then he will always be with me inside my heart.

Acknowledgments

Although it had always been my intention to write about my work at Sing Sing, my abrupt departure left me so devastated that for two years I was unable to do so. Then Susan Gehringer, one of my friends from my West Point days, gave me the prod I needed to unleash the story that was waiting to be told. From that moment on, with that old gospel song *I Love to Tell the Story* echoing ceaselessly in my head, the story practically told itself, coming out as a torrential downpour. Once it was somewhat complete, Margaret Starbird, another friend and author from West Point, helped me begin the editing process and gave me lots of constructive suggestions. In addition, numerous members of my family behind bars lent their enthusiastic support throughout the entire writing process, especially Rob, Dave, and Ricky, as well as Pat, Mark, Steve, and Johnny, who wrote testimonials.

Ever since Maryknoll, a Catholic Mission Society, was founded over a century ago just up the hill from Sing Sing, ministering to the men of Sing Sing has been an extension of their mission. I heard stories from some of the older priests of how they used to celebrate mass and hear confessions in the old Death House for men awaiting their execution. I will always be particularly grateful to former lay missioners Leo and Andrea Goicochea, who helped to cultivate our Hispanic ministry and also "hoodwinked" Father José Aramburu to get on board. When my mother was dying of cancer he filled in for me so I could spend those priceless last weeks with her in Wisconsin. Numerous other Maryknoll priests and sisters assisted during the years I worked there, some as chapel volunteers and others who visited and corresponded with the men and kept them in their prayers. One of them was instrumental in helping an unjustly convicted man to be set free. The overall ministry at Sing Sing was tremendously enriched and continually inspired by the mission of Maryknoll and by all the other volunteers who assisted me in "proclaiming liberty to captives" in Sing Sing prison. It was through all of us working together that we were able to create a refuge in the midst of the hell known as Sing Sing.

About the Author

Father Ronald Lemmert grew up in Wisconsin, the son of a Baptist minister. He graduated from the University of Colorado with a bachelor's degree in music, specializing in organ performance. After completing his master's degree in the same field from Southern Methodist University, he was drafted into the Army in 1970 and was sent in 1971 to the United States Military Academy at West Point, New York, to be the organist-choirmaster at the Catholic chapel. It was there that he converted to Catholicism and subsequently left to enter St. Joseph's Seminary and was ordained a priest for the Archdiocese of New York in 1979.

After several parish assignments he became a part-time chaplain at Westchester County Jail in 1994, then a full-time chaplain at Sing Sing Correctional Facility in 1995. From 2008 to 2011 he also served at Bedford Hills Correctional Facility for women. Since his retirement from the New York State Department of Correctional Services in 2011 he has been serving as Catholic chaplain at Phelps Memorial Northwell Hospital in Sleepy Hollow, New York. He also celebrates mass for the Religious of the Sacred Heart of Mary at Marymount Convent in Tarrytown, New York; Holy Name of Mary Parish in Croton-on-Hudson; and St. Teresa's Parish in Briarcliff, New York. He is one of the founders of Catholic Whistleblowers, a group of people who have blown the whistle on the clergy sex-abuse scandal, and he has also been involved in Restorative Justice Healing Circles for the survivors of clergy sex abuse under the sponsorship of Voice of the Faithful. He still lives at My Father's House, which he founded as a halfway house for ex-offenders in Peekskill, New York, in 1996.